THE
POWER
OF GOD

THE
POWER
OF GOD

Compiled by Eugene Carvalho

To the Body of Christ.
May this compilation bless you richly!
With love…

TABLE OF CONTENTS

PURPOSE & ACKNOWLEDGEMENTS   9

Chapter 1
THE POWER OF GOD   11

Chapter 2
HIS POWER IN THE OLD TESTAMENT   13

Chapter 3
HIS POWER IN THE NEW TESTAMENT   51

DAILY FAITH CONFESSIONS   92
PRAYER FOR SALVATION   95
ABOUT THE AUTHOR   96
BOOKS BY EUGENE IN ENGLISH   97
BOOKS BY EUGENE IN SPANISH   100
NOTES   101

PURPOSE AND ACKNOWLEDGEMENTS

The infallible Word of God for faith and conduct informs us that the Holy Spirit gives gifts to men and women of the Body of Christ. It states: "the gifts edify the body for the building up of the saints" (Eph. 4:12). I hope the talents and gifts the Lord has given me will be a blessing to someone else through the reading of this compilation.

I am grateful for the love I have received from family members, especially my wife Mercedes. I am also grateful for the knowledge, wisdom and love of many pastors, teachers, and saints that the Lord has used to bless me. Lastly, I must not forget a special thank you to my friend Kathryn Regan for proofreading this material.

THE POWER OF GOD

The difference between the power of God and the presence of God are sometimes misunderstood by the body of Christ. I hear misleading statements regarding the two of them all the time on Christian radio and preached from many pulpits. Statements like, I could feel the presence of God in the service. Or the presence of God showed up. You cannot feel the presence of God.

It's vital to understand, "God's presence is His attributes and nature. The power is the overflow of the life of the Messiah. You cannot feel the presence of God. The presence of God is within you. God's presence is not felt. It is known. The Bible says, "Be still and know that I am God." It's the power of God we feel. We can lay hands on people and they receive deliverance and healing. We cannot lay hands on someone to be saved. That's the difference between His power and His presence. His power is totally separate. He is with you, in you, and on you. He is with you before you get saved to convict you of sin. His presence is in you when you get saved. And He's on you for service."[1] The Bible says, "But ye shall receive power, after that the Holy Ghost is come upon you: and ye shall be witnesses unto me both in Jerusalem, and in all Judaea, and in Samaria, and unto the uttermost part of the earth" (Ac. 1:8 KJV).

Let's investigate this word power to see if we can get a better understanding. "Power – the ability

---

[1] Quote by Benny Hinn

or strength to perform an activity or deed. Power is sometimes used with the word authority. If power suggests physical strength, authority suggests a moral right or privilege.

One can have power to perform a task but not have authority to do it. Jesus Christ had both power and authority (Luke 4:36), and He bestowed these upon His followers (Luke 10:19)."[2]

Let's look at those two verses. "And amazement came upon them all, and they began talking with one another saying, 'What is this message? For with authority and power He commands the unclean spirits and they come out'" (Luke 4:36). Along with, "Behold, I have given you authority to tread on serpents and scorpions, and over all the power of the enemy, and nothing will injure you" (Luke 10:19).

With that being said, let's investigate the infallible scriptures that discuss the Power of God.

---

[2] Ronald F. Youngblood, *Nelson's New Illustrated Bible Dictionary*, Nashville, 1995, P. 1021

HIS POWER IN THE OLD TESTAMENT

IN THE BOOK OF EXODUS

My Power and in Order to Proclaim My Name

"Then the Lord said to Moses, 'Rise up early in the morning and stand before Pharaoh and say to him, 'Thus says the Lord, the God of the Hebrews, "Let My people go, that they may serve Me. For this time I will send all My plagues on you and your servants and your people, so that you may know that there is no one like Me in all the earth. For if by now I had put forth My hand and struck you and your people with pestilence, you would then have been cut off from the earth. But, indeed, for this reason I have allowed you to remain, in order to show you My power and in order to proclaim My name through all the earth. Still you exalt yourself against My people by not letting them go. Behold, about this time tomorrow, I will send a very heavy hail, such as has not been seen in Egypt from the day it was founded until now. Now therefore send, bring your livestock and whatever you have in the field to safety. Every man and beast that is found in the field and is not brought home, when the hail comes down on them, will die.'"' The one among the servants of Pharaoh who feared the word of the Lord made his servants and his livestock flee into the houses; but he who paid no regard to the word of the Lord left his servants and his livestock in the field" (Ex 9:13-21).[3]

The Great Power Which the Lord Had Used

"Thus the Lord saved Israel that day from the hand of the Egyptians, and Israel saw the Egyptians dead on the seashore. When Israel saw the great power which the Lord had used against the Egyptians, the people feared the Lord, and they believed in the Lord and in His servant Moses" (Ex. 14:30-31).

Your Right Hand, O Lord, Is Majestic in Power

"Then Moses and the sons of Israel sang this song to the Lord, and said, 'I will sing to the Lord, for He is highly exalted; The horse and its rider He has hurled into the sea. The Lord is my strength and song, And He has become my salvation; This is my God, and I will praise Him; My father's God, and I will extol Him. The Lord is a warrior; The Lord is His name. Pharaoh's chariots and his army He has cast into the sea; And the choicest of his officers are drowned in the Red Sea. The deeps cover them; They went down into the depths like a stone. Your right hand, O Lord, is majestic in power, Your right hand, O Lord, shatters the enemy'" (Ex. 15:1-6).

---

[3] All Scripture quotations, unless otherwise noted, are from the *New American Standard Bible.*

With Great Power and with a Mighty Hand

"Then Moses entreated the Lord his God, and said, 'O Lord, why does Your anger burn against Your people whom You have brought out from the land of Egypt with great power and with a mighty hand? Why should the Egyptians speak, saying, "With evil intent He brought them out to kill them in the mountains and to destroy them from the face of the earth"? Turn from Your burning anger and change Your mind about doing harm to Your people. Remember Abraham, Isaac, and Israel, Your servants to whom You swore by Yourself, and said to them, 'I will multiply your descendants as the stars of the heavens, and all this land of which I have spoken I will give to your descendants, and they shall inherit it forever.'" So the Lord changed His mind about the harm which He said He would do to His people" (Ex. 32:11-14).

IN THE BOOK OF NUMBERS

Let the Power of the Lord Be Great

"But Moses said to the Lord, 'Then the Egyptians will hear of it, for by Your strength You brought up this people from their midst, and they will tell it to the inhabitants of this land. They have heard that You, O Lord, are in the midst of this people, for You, O Lord, are seen eye to eye, while Your cloud stands over them; and You go before them in a pillar of cloud by day and in a pillar of fire by night. Now if You slay this people as one man, then the nations who have heard of Your fame will say, "Because the Lord could not bring this people into the land which He promised them by oath, therefore He slaughtered them in the wilderness." But now, I pray, let the power of the Lord be great, just as You have declared, "The Lord is slow to anger and abundant in lovingkindness, forgiving iniquity and transgression; but He will by no means clear the guilty, visiting the iniquity of the fathers on the children to the third and the fourth generations.' Pardon, I pray, the iniquity of this people according to the greatness of Your lovingkindness, just as You also have forgiven this people, from Egypt even until now'" (Nu. 14:13-19).

IN THE BOOK OF DEUTERONOMY

His Great Power

"Indeed, ask now concerning the former days which were before you, since the day that God created man on the earth, and inquire from one end of the heavens to the other. Has anything been done like this great thing, or has anything been heard like it? Has any people heard the voice of God speaking from the midst of the fire, as you have heard it, and survived? Or has a god tried to go to take for himself a nation from within another nation by trials, by signs and wonders and by war and by a mighty hand and by an outstretched arm and by great terrors, as the Lord your God did for you in Egypt before your eyes? To you it was shown that you might know that the Lord, He is God; there is no other besides Him. Out of the heavens He let you hear His voice to discipline you; and on earth He let you see His great fire, and you heard His words from the midst of the fire. Because He loved your fathers, therefore He chose their descendants after them. And He personally brought you from Egypt by His great power, driving out from before you nations greater and mightier than you, to bring you in and to give you their land for an inheritance, as it is today. Know therefore today, and take it to your heart, that the Lord, He is God in heaven above and on the earth below; there is no other" (Dt. 4:32-39).

God Gives You Power to Make Wealth

"Beware that you do not forget the Lord your God by not keeping His commandments and His ordinances and His statutes which I am commanding you today; otherwise, when you have eaten and are satisfied, and have built good houses and lived in them, and when your herds and your flocks multiply, and your silver and gold multiply, and all that you have multiplies, then your heart will become proud and you will forget the Lord your God who brought you out from the land of Egypt, out of the house of slavery. He led you through the great and terrible wilderness, with its fiery serpents and scorpions and thirsty ground where there was no water; He brought water for you out of the rock of flint. In the wilderness He fed you manna which your fathers did not know, that He might humble you and that He might test you, to do good for you in the end. Otherwise, you may say in your heart, 'My power and the strength of my hand made me this wealth.' But you shall remember the Lord your God, for it is He who is giving you power to make wealth, that He may confirm His covenant which He swore to your fathers, as it is this day. It shall come about if you ever forget the Lord your God and go after other gods and serve them and worship them, I testify against you today that you will surely perish. Like the nations that the Lord makes to perish before you, so you shall perish; because you would not listen to the voice of the Lord your God" (Dt. 8:11-20).

Your Great Power and Your Outstretched Arm

"So I fell down before the Lord the forty days and nights, which I did because the Lord had said He would destroy you. I prayed to the Lord and said, 'O Lord God, do not destroy Your people, even Your inheritance, whom You have redeemed through Your greatness, whom You have brought out of Egypt with a mighty hand. Remember Your servants, Abraham, Isaac, and Jacob; do not look at the stubbornness of this people or at their wickedness or their sin. Otherwise the land from which You brought us may say, "Because the Lord was not able to bring them into the land which He had promised them and because He hated them He has brought them out to slay them in the wilderness." Yet they are Your people, even Your inheritance, whom You have brought out by Your great power and Your outstretched arm'" (Dt. 9:25-29).

All the Mighty Power and for All the Great Terror

Now Joshua the son of Nun was filled with the spirit of wisdom, for Moses had laid his hands on him; and the sons of Israel listened to him and did as the Lord had commanded Moses. Since that time no prophet has risen in Israel like Moses, whom the Lord knew face to face, for all the signs and wonders which the Lord sent him to perform in the land of Egypt against Pharaoh, all his servants, and all his land, and for all the mighty power and for all the great terror which Moses performed in the sight of all Israel" (Dt. 34:9-12).

The Power of All the Kingdoms

"Thereafter Samuel called the people together to the Lord at Mizpah; and he said to the sons of Israel, 'Thus says the Lord, the God of Israel, "I brought Israel up from Egypt, and I delivered you from the hand of the Egyptians and from the power of all the kingdoms that were oppressing you." But you have today rejected your God, who delivers you from all your calamities and your distresses; yet you have said, "No, but set a king over us!" Now therefore, present yourselves before the Lord by your tribes and by your clans" (1Sa. 10:17-19).

IN THE BOOK OF 2 KINGS

From the Land of Egypt with Great Power

"To this day they do according to the earlier customs: they do not fear the Lord, nor do they follow their statutes or their ordinances or the law, or the commandments which the Lord commanded the sons of Jacob, whom He named Israel; with whom the Lord made a covenant and commanded them, saying, 'You shall not fear other gods, nor bow down yourselves to them nor serve them nor sacrifice to them. But the Lord, who brought you up from the land of Egypt with great power and with an outstretched arm, Him you shall fear, and to Him you shall bow yourselves down, and to Him you shall sacrifice. The statutes and the ordinances and the law and the commandment which He wrote for you, you shall observe to do forever; and you shall not fear other gods. The covenant that I have made with you, you shall not forget, nor shall you fear other gods. But the Lord your God you shall fear; and He will deliver you from the hand of all your enemies.' However, they did not listen, but they did according to their earlier custom. So while these nations feared the Lord, they also served their idols; their children likewise and their grandchildren, as their fathers did, so they do to this day" (2Ki. 17:34-41).

IN THE BOOK OF 1 CHRONICLES

In Your Hand Is Power and Might

"So David blessed the Lord in the sight of all the assembly; and David said, 'Blessed are You, O Lord God of Israel our father, forever and ever. Yours, O Lord, is the greatness and the power and the glory and the victory and the majesty, indeed everything that is in the heavens and the earth;

Yours is the dominion, O Lord, and You exalt Yourself as head over all. Both riches and honor come from You, and You rule over all, and in Your hand is power and might; and it lies in Your hand to make great and to strengthen everyone. Now therefore, our God, we thank You, and praise Your glorious name'" (1Ch. 29:10-13).

IN THE BOOK OF 2 CHRONICLES

Power and Might Are in Your Hand

"Then Jehoshaphat stood in the assembly of Judah and Jerusalem, in the house of the Lord before the new court, and he said, 'O Lord, the God of our fathers, are You not God in the heavens? And are You not ruler over all the kingdoms of the nations? Power and might are in Your hand so that no one can stand against You. Did You not, O our God, drive out the inhabitants of this land before Your people Israel and give it to the descendants of Abraham Your friend forever? They have lived in it, and have built You a sanctuary there for Your name, saying, "Should evil come upon us, the sword, or judgment, or pestilence, or famine, we will stand before this house and before You (for Your name is in this house) and cry to You in our distress, and You will hear and deliver us." Now behold, the sons of Ammon and Moab and Mount Seir, whom You did not let Israel invade when they came out of the land of Egypt (they turned aside from them and did not destroy them), see how they are rewarding us by coming to drive us out from Your possession which You have given us as an inheritance. O our God, will

You not judge them? For we are powerless before this great multitude who are coming against us; nor do we know what to do, but our eyes are on You'" (2Ch. 20:5-12).

God Has Power to Help and to Bring Down

"Moreover, Amaziah assembled Judah and appointed them according to their fathers' households under commanders of thousands and commanders of hundreds throughout Judah and Benjamin; and he took a census of those from twenty years old and upward and found them to be 300,000 choice men, able to go to war and handle spear and shield. He hired also 100,000 valiant warriors out of Israel for one hundred talents of silver. But a man of God came to him saying, 'O king, do not let the army of Israel go with you, for the Lord is not with Israel nor with any of the sons of Ephraim. But if you do go, do it, be strong for the battle; yet God will bring you down before the enemy, for God has power to help and to bring down.' Amaziah said to the man of God, 'But what shall we do for the hundred talents which I have given to the troops of Israel?' And the man of God answered, "The Lord has much more to give you than this.' Then Amaziah dismissed them, the troops which came to him from Ephraim, to go home; so their anger burned against Judah and they returned home in fierce anger" (2Ch. 25:5-10).

Chapter Two

Wage War with Great Power

"Now he went out and warred against the Philistines, and broke down the wall of Gath and the wall of Jabneh and the wall of Ashdod; and he built cities in the area of Ashdod and among the Philistines. God helped him against the Philistines, and against the Arabians who lived in Gur-baal, and the Meunites. The Ammonites also gave tribute to Uzziah, and his fame extended to the border of Egypt, for he became very strong. Moreover, Uzziah built towers in Jerusalem at the Corner Gate and at the Valley Gate and at the corner buttress and fortified them. He built towers in the wilderness and hewed many cisterns, for he had much livestock, both in the lowland and in the plain. He also had plowmen and vinedressers in the hill country and the fertile fields, for he loved the soil. Moreover, Uzziah had an army ready for battle, which entered combat by divisions according to the number of their muster, prepared by Jeiel the scribe and Maaseiah the official, under the direction of Hananiah, one of the king's officers. The total number of the heads of the households, of valiant warriors, was 2,600. Under their direction was an elite army of 307,500, who could wage war with great power, to help the king against the enemy. Moreover, Uzziah prepared for all the army shields, spears, helmets, body armor, bows and sling stones. In Jerusalem he made engines of war invented by skillful men to be on the towers and on the corners for the purpose of shooting arrows and great stones. Hence his fame spread afar, for he was marvelously helped until he was strong" (2Ch. 26:6-15).

Chapter Two

IN THE BOOK OF EZRA

His Power and His Anger

"Then I proclaimed a fast there at the river of Ahava, that we might humble ourselves before our God to seek from Him a safe journey for us, our little ones, and all our possessions. For I was ashamed to request from the king troops and horsemen to protect us from the enemy on the way, because we had said to the king, 'The hand of our God is favorably disposed to all those who seek Him, but His power and His anger are against all those who forsake Him.' So we fasted and sought our God concerning this matter, and He listened to our entreaty" (Ezr. 8:21-23).

IN THE BOOK OF NEHEMIAH

Your People Whom You Redeemed by Your Power

"When I heard these words, I sat down and wept and mourned for days; and I was fasting and praying before the God of heaven. I said, 'I beseech You, O Lord God of heaven, the great and awesome God, who preserves the covenant and lovingkindness for those who love Him and keep His commandments, let Your ear now be attentive and Your eyes open to hear the prayer of Your servant which I am praying before You now, day and night, on behalf of the sons of Israel Your servants, confessing the sins of the sons of Israel which we have sinned against You; I and my father's house have sinned. We have acted very corruptly against You and have not kept the commandments, nor the statutes, nor the ordinances which You commanded Your servant Moses. Remember the word which You commanded Your servant Moses, saying, "If you are unfaithful I will scatter you among the peoples; but if you return to Me and keep My commandments and do them, though those of you who have been scattered were in the most remote part of the heavens, I will gather them from there and will bring them to the place where I have chosen to cause My name to dwell." They are Your servants and Your people whom You redeemed by Your great power and by Your strong hand. O Lord, I beseech You, may Your ear be attentive to the prayer of Your servant and the prayer of Your servants who delight to revere Your name, and make Your servant successful today and grant him compassion before this man.' Now I was the cupbearer to the king" (Ne. 1:4-11).

IN THE BOOK OF JOB

In War from the Power of the Sword

"Behold, how happy is the man whom God reproves, So do not despise the discipline of the Almighty. For He inflicts pain, and gives relief; He wounds, and His hands also heal. From six troubles He will deliver you, Even in seven evil will not touch you. In famine He will redeem you from death, And in war from the power of the sword. You will be hidden from the scourge of the tongue, And you will not be afraid of violence when it comes. You will laugh at violence and famine, And you will not be afraid of wild beasts. For you will be in league with the stones of the field, And the beasts of the field will be at peace with you. You will know that your tent is secure, For you will visit your abode and fear no loss. You will know also that your descendants will be many, And your offspring as the grass of the earth. You will come to the grave in full vigor, Like the stacking of grain in its season. Behold this; we have investigated it, and so it is. Hear it, and know for yourself" (Job 5:17-27).

The Power of Their Transgression

"Then Bildad the Shuhite answered, 'How long will you say these things, And the words of your mouth be a mighty wind? Does God pervert justice? Or does the Almighty pervert what is right? If your sons sinned against Him, Then He delivered them into the power of their transgression. If you would seek God And implore the compassion of the Almighty, If you are pure and upright, Surely now He would rouse Himself for you And restore your righteous estate. Though your beginning was insignificant, Yet your end will increase greatly'" (Job 8:1-7).

A Matter of Power

"God will not turn back His anger; Beneath Him crouch the helpers of Rahab. How then can I answer Him, And choose my words before Him? For though I were right, I could not answer; I would have to implore the mercy of my judge. If I called and He answered me, I could not believe that He was listening to my voice. For He bruises me with a tempest And multiplies my wounds without cause. He will not allow me to get my breath, But saturates me with bitterness. If it is a matter of power, behold, He is the strong one! And if it is a matter of justice, who can summon Him? Though I am righteous, my mouth will condemn me; Though I am guiltless, He will declare me guilty. I am guiltless; I do not take notice of myself; I despise my life. It is all one; therefore I say, 'He destroys the guiltless and the wicked.' If the scourge kills suddenly, He mocks the despair of the innocent. The earth is given into the hand of the wicked; He covers the faces of its judges. If it is not He, then who is it" (Job 9:13-24)?

You Would Show Your Power Against Me

"Your hands fashioned and made me altogether, And would You destroy me? Remember now, that You have made me as clay; And would You turn me into dust again? Did You not pour me out like milk And curdle me like cheese; Clothe me with skin and flesh, And knit me together with bones and sinews? You have granted me life and lovingkindness; And Your care has preserved my spirit. Yet these things You have concealed in Your heart; I know that this is within You: If I sin, then You would take note of me, And would not acquit me of my guilt. If I am wicked, woe to me! And if I am righteous, I dare not lift up my head. I am sated with disgrace and conscious of my misery. Should my head be lifted up, You would hunt me like a lion; And again You would show Your power against me. You renew Your witnesses against me And increase

Your anger toward me; Hardship after hardship is with me" (Job 10:8-17).

By the Greatness of His Power

"Then Job replied, 'Even today my complaint is rebellion; His hand is heavy despite my groaning. Oh that I knew where I might find Him, That I might come to His seat! I would present my case before Him And fill my mouth with arguments. I would learn the words which He would answer, And perceive what He would say to me. Would He contend with me by the greatness of His power? No, surely He would pay attention to me. There the upright would reason with Him; And I would be delivered forever from my Judge'" (Job 23:1-7).

He Drags off the Valiant by His power

"They are insignificant on the surface of the water; Their portion is cursed on the earth. They do not turn toward the vineyards. Drought and heat consume the snow waters, So does Sheol those who have sinned. A mother will forget him; The worm feeds sweetly till he is no longer remembered. And wickedness will be broken like a tree. He wrongs the barren woman And does no good for the widow. But He drags off the valiant by His power; He rises, but no one has assurance of life. He provides them with security, and they are supported; And His eyes are on their ways. They are exalted a little while, then they are gone; Moreover, they are brought low and like everything gathered up; Even like the heads of grain they are cut off. Now if it is not so, who can prove me a liar, And make my speech worthless" (Job 24:18-25)?

He Quieted the Sea with His Power

"The departed spirits tremble Under the waters and their inhabitants. Naked is Sheol before Him, And Abaddon has no covering. He stretches out the north over empty space And hangs the earth on nothing. He wraps up the waters in His clouds, And the cloud does not burst under them. He obscures the face of the full moon And spreads His cloud over it. He has inscribed a circle on the surface of the waters At the boundary of light and darkness. The pillars of heaven tremble And are amazed at His rebuke. He quieted the sea with His power, And by His understanding He shattered Rahab. By His breath the heavens are cleared; His hand has pierced the fleeing serpent. Behold, these are the fringes of His ways; And how faint a word we hear of Him! But His mighty thunder, who can understand" (Job 26:5-14)?

I Will Instruct You in the Power of God

"May my enemy be as the wicked And my opponent as the unjust. For what is the hope of the godless when he is cut off, When God requires his life? Will God hear his cry When distress comes upon him? Will he take delight in the Almighty? Will he call on God at all times? I will instruct you in the power of God; What is with the Almighty I will not conceal. Behold, all of you have seen it; Why then do you act foolishly" (Job 27:7-12)?

Chapter Two

Behold, God Is Exalted in His Power

"But you were full of judgment on the wicked; Judgment and justice take hold of you. Beware that wrath does not entice you to scoffing; And do not let the greatness of the ransom turn you aside. Will your riches keep you from distress, Or all the forces of your strength? Do not long for the night, When people vanish in their place. Be careful, do not turn to evil, For you have preferred this to affliction. Behold, God is exalted in His power; Who is a teacher like Him? Who has appointed Him His way, And who has said, You have done wrong'" (Job 36:17-23)?

Exalted in Power and He Will Not Do Violence

"Now men do not see the light which is bright in the skies; But the wind has passed and cleared them. Out of the north comes golden splendor; Around God is awesome majesty. The Almighty—we cannot find Him; He is exalted in power And He will not do violence to justice and abundant righteousness. Therefore men fear Him; He does not regard any who are wise of heart" (Job 37:21-24).

IN THE BOOK OF PSLAMS

We Will Sing and Praise Your Power

"For the king trusts in the Lord, and through the lovingkindness of the Most High he will not be shaken. Your hand will find out all your enemies;

Your right hand will find out those who hate you. You will make them as a fiery oven in the time of your anger; The Lord will swallow them up in His wrath, and fire will devour them. Their offspring You will destroy from the earth, And their descendants from among the sons of men. Though they intended evil against You and devised a plot, They will not succeed. For You will make them turn their back; You will aim with Your bowstrings at their faces. Be exalted, O Lord, in Your strength; We will sing and praise Your power" (Ps. 21:7-13).

Vindicate Me by Your Power

"Save me, O God, by Your name, and vindicate me by Your power. Hear my prayer, O God; Give ear to the words of my mouth. For strangers have risen against me And violent men have sought my life; they have not set God before them" (Ps. 54:1-3).

Scatter Them by Your Power, and Bring Them Down

"Because of his strength I will watch for You, For God is my stronghold. My God in His lovingkindness will meet me; God will let me look triumphantly upon my foes. Do not slay them, or my people will forget; scatter them by Your power, and bring them down, O Lord, our shield. On account of the sin of their mouth and the words of their lips, let them even be caught in their pride, And on account of curses and lies which they utter. Destroy them in wrath, destroy them that they may be no more; that men may know that God rules in Jacob To the ends of the earth. They return at evening, they howl like a dog, and go around the city. They wander about for food and growl if they are not satisfied" (Ps. 59:9-15).

Power Belongs to God

"Once God has spoken; twice I have heard this: That power belongs to God; and lovingkindness is Yours, O Lord, For You recompense a man according to his work" (Ps. 62:11-12).

To See Your Power and Your Glory

"O God, You are my God; I shall seek You earnestly; my soul thirsts for You, my flesh yearns for You, In a dry and weary land where there is no water. Thus I have seen You in the sanctuary, To see Your power and Your glory. Because Your lovingkindness is better than life, my lips will praise You. So I will bless You as long as I live; I will lift up my hands in Your name. My soul is satisfied as with marrow and fatness, and my mouth offers praises with joyful lips" (Ps. 63:1-5).

Because of the Greatness of Your Power Your Enemies Will Give Feigned Obedience to You

"Shout joyfully to God, all the earth; sing the glory of His name; Make His praise glorious. Say to God, 'How awesome are Your works! Because of the greatness of Your power Your enemies will give feigned obedience to You. All the earth will worship

You, and will sing praises to You; they will sing praises to Your name'" (Ps. 66:1-4).

He Gives Strength and Power to the People

"Sing to God, O kingdoms of the earth, sing praises to the Lord, to Him who rides upon the highest heavens, which are from ancient times; behold, He speaks forth with His voice, a mighty voice. Ascribe strength to God; His majesty is over Israel and His strength is in the skies. O God, You are awesome from Your sanctuary. The God of Israel Himself gives strength and power to the people. Blessed be God" (Ps. 68:32-35)!

Your Power to All Who Are to Come

"O God, You have taught me from my youth, and I still declare Your wondrous deeds. And even when I am old and gray, O God, do not forsake me, until I declare Your strength to this generation, Your power to all who are to come. For Your righteousness, O God, reaches to the heavens, You who have done great things; O God, who is like You? You who have shown me many troubles and distresses will revive me again, and will bring me up again from the depths of the earth. May You increase my greatness and turn to comfort me" (Ps. 71:17-21).

By Your Power You Have Redeemed Your People

"I shall remember the deeds of the Lord; surely I will remember Your wonders of old. I will meditate on all Your work and muse on Your deeds.

Your way, O God, is holy; what god is great like our God? You are the God who works wonders; You have made known Your strength among the peoples. You have by Your power redeemed Your people, the sons of Jacob and Joseph" (Ps. 77:11-15).

By His Power He Directed the South Wind

"Therefore the Lord heard and was full of wrath; and a fire was kindled against Jacob and anger also mounted against Israel, because they did not believe in God And did not trust in His salvation. Yet He commanded the clouds above and opened the doors of heaven; He rained down manna upon them to eat and gave them food from heaven. Man did eat the bread of angels; He sent them food in abundance. He caused the east wind to blow in the heavens and by His power He directed the south wind. When He rained meat upon them like the dust, even winged fowl like the sand of the seas, then He let them fall in the midst of their camp, round about their dwellings. So they ate and were well filled, and their desire He gave to them. Before they had satisfied their desire, while their food was in their mouths, the anger of God rose against them and killed some of their stoutest ones, and subdued the choice men of Israel. In spite of all this they still sinned and did not believe in His wonderful works. So He brought their days to an end in futility and their years in sudden terror" (Ps. 78:21-33).

They Did Not Remember His Power

"How often they rebelled against Him in the wilderness And grieved Him in the desert! Again and again they tempted God, and pained the Holy One of Israel. They did not remember His power, the day when He redeemed them from the adversary, when He performed His signs in Egypt and His marvels in the field of Zoan, and turned their rivers to blood, and their streams, they could not drink. He sent among them swarms of flies which devoured them, and frogs which destroyed them. He gave also their crops to the grasshopper and the product of their labor to the locust. He destroyed their vines with hailstones and their sycamore trees with frost. He gave over their cattle also to the hailstones and their herds to bolts of lightning. He sent upon them His burning anger, fury and indignation and trouble, a band of destroying angels. He leveled a path for His anger; He did not spare their soul from death, but gave over their life to the plague, and smote all the firstborn in Egypt, the first issue of their virility in the tents of Ham. But He led forth His own people like sheep and guided them in the wilderness like a flock; He led them safely, so that they did not fear; But the sea engulfed their enemies" (Ps. 78:40-53).

By Your Power Preserve Those Who Are Doomed

"Do not remember the iniquities of our forefathers against us; let Your compassion come quickly to meet us, for we are brought very low. Help us, O God of our salvation, for the glory of

Your name; and deliver us and forgive our sins for Your name's sake. Why should the nations say, 'Where is their God?' Let there be known among the nations in our sight, vengeance for the blood of Your servants which has been shed. Let the groaning of the prisoner come before You; according to the greatness of Your power preserve those who are doomed to die. And return to our neighbors sevenfold into their bosom the reproach with which they have reproached You, O Lord. So we Your people and the sheep of Your pasture will give thanks to You forever; to all generations we will tell of Your praise" (Ps. 79:8-13).

Stir up Your Power and Come to Save Us

"Oh, give ear, Shepherd of Israel, You who lead Joseph like a flock; You who are enthroned above the cherubim, shine forth! Before Ephraim and Benjamin and Manasseh, stir up Your power and come to save us! O God, restore us and cause Your face to shine upon us, and we will be saved" (Ps. 80:1-3).

The Power of Your Anger and Your Fury

"For we have been consumed by Your anger and by Your wrath we have been dismayed. You have placed our iniquities before You, our secret sins in the light of Your presence. For all our days have declined in Your fury; we have finished our years like a sigh. As for the days of our life, they contain seventy years, or if due to strength, eighty years, yet their pride is but labor and sorrow; for soon it is gone and we fly away. Who understands the power of Your anger and Your fury, according to the fear that is due You? So teach us to number our days, that we may present to You a heart of wisdom" (Ps. 90:7-12).

That He Might Make His Power Known

"We have sinned like our fathers, we have committed iniquity, we have behaved wickedly. Our fathers in Egypt did not understand Your wonders; they did not remember Your abundant kindnesses, but rebelled by the sea, at the Red Sea. Nevertheless He saved them for the sake of His name, that He might make His power known. Thus He rebuked the Red Sea and it dried up, and He led them through the deeps, as through the wilderness. So He saved them from the hand of the one who hated them, and redeemed them from the hand of the enemy. The waters covered their adversaries; not one of them was left. Then they believed His words; they sang His praise" (Ps. 106:6-12).

People Will Volunteer in the Day of Your Power

"The Lord says to my Lord: 'Sit at My right hand until I make Your enemies a footstool for Your feet.' The Lord will stretch forth Your strong scepter from Zion, saying, 'Rule in the midst of Your enemies.' Your people will volunteer freely in the day of Your power; in holy array, from the womb of the dawn, Your youth are to You as the dew" (Ps. 110:1-3).

Chapter Two

Made Known to His People the Power of His Works

"Praise the Lord! I will give thanks to the Lord with all my heart, in the company of the upright and in the assembly. Great are the works of the Lord; they are studied by all who delight in them. Splendid and majestic is His work, and His righteousness endures forever. He has made His wonders to be remembered; the Lord is gracious and compassionate. He has given food to those who fear Him; He will remember His covenant forever. He has made known to His people the power of His works, in giving them the heritage of the nations. The works of His hands are truth and justice; all His precepts are sure. They are upheld forever and ever; they are performed in truth and uprightness. He has sent redemption to His people; He has ordained His covenant forever; Holy and awesome is His name. The fear of the Lord is the beginning of wisdom; a good understanding have all those who do His commandments; His praise endures forever" (Ps. 111:1-10).

The Power of Your Awesome Acts and Greatness

"I will extol You, my God, O King, and I will bless Your name forever and ever. Every day I will bless You, and I will praise Your name forever and ever. Great is the Lord, and highly to be praised, and His greatness is unsearchable. One generation shall praise Your works to another, and shall declare Your mighty acts. On the glorious splendor of Your majesty and on Your wonderful works, I will meditate. Men shall speak of the power of Your awesome acts, and I will tell of Your greatness. They shall eagerly utter the memory of Your abundant goodness and will shout joyfully of Your righteousness" (Ps. 145:1-7).

The Glory of Your Kingdom and Talk of Your Power

"The Lord is gracious and merciful; Slow to anger and great in lovingkindness. The Lord is good to all, And His mercies are over all His works. All Your works shall give thanks to You, O Lord, And Your godly ones shall bless You. They shall speak of the glory of Your kingdom And talk of Your power; To make known to the sons of men Your mighty acts And the glory of the majesty of Your kingdom. Your kingdom is an everlasting kingdom, And Your dominion endures throughout all generations" (Ps. 145:8-13).

IN THE BOOK OF PROVERBS

When It Is in Your Power to Do It

"Do not withhold good from those to whom it is due, When it is in your power to do it. Do not say to your neighbor, 'Go, and come back, And tomorrow I will give it,' When you have it with you" (Pr. 3:27-28).

IN THE BOOK OF ISAIAH

Chapter Two

The Lord Spoke to Me with Mighty Power

"For thus the Lord spoke to me with mighty power and instructed me not to walk in the way of this people, saying, 'You are not to say, "It is a conspiracy!" In regard to all that this people call a conspiracy, And you are not to fear what they fear or be in dread of it. It is the Lord of hosts whom you should regard as holy. And He shall be your fear, And He shall be your dread. Then He shall become a sanctuary; But to both the houses of Israel, a stone to strike and a rock to stumble over, And a snare and a trap for the inhabitants of Jerusalem. Many will stumble over them, Then they will fall and be broken; They will even be snared and caught'" (Is. 8:11-15).

By the Power of My Hand

"So it will be that when the Lord has completed all His work on Mount Zion and on Jerusalem, He will say, 'I will punish the fruit of the arrogant heart of the king of Assyria and the pomp of his haughtiness.' For he has said, 'By the power of my hand and by my wisdom I did this, For I have understanding; And I removed the boundaries of the peoples And plundered their treasures, And like a mighty man I brought down their inhabitants, And my hand reached to the riches of the peoples like a nest, And as one gathers abandoned eggs, I gathered all the earth; And there was not one that flapped its wing or opened its beak or chirped'" (Is. 10:12-14).

His Might and the Strength of His Power

"Do you not know? Have you not heard? Has it not been declared to you from the beginning? Have you not understood from the foundations of the earth? It is He who sits above the circle of the earth, And its inhabitants are like grasshoppers, Who stretches out the heavens like a curtain And spreads them out like a tent to dwell in. He it is who reduces rulers to nothing, Who makes the judges of the earth meaningless. Scarcely have they been planted, Scarcely have they been sown, Scarcely has their stock taken root in the earth, But He merely blows on them, and they wither, And the storm carries them away like stubble. 'To whom then will you liken Me That I would be his equal?' says the Holy One. Lift up your eyes on high And see who has created these stars, The One who leads forth their host by number, He calls them all by name; Because of the greatness of His might and the strength of His power, Not one of them is missing" (Is. 40:21-26).

To Him Who Lacks Might He Increases Power

"Why do you say, O Jacob, and assert, O Israel, 'My way is hidden from the Lord, And the justice due me escapes the notice of my God'? Do you not know? Have you not heard? The Everlasting God, the Lord, the Creator of the ends of the earth Does not become weary or tired. His understanding is inscrutable. He gives strength to the weary, And to him who lacks might He increases power. Though youths grow weary and tired, And vigorous young men stumble badly, Yet those who wait for the Lord Will gain new strength; They will mount up with wings like eagles, They will run and not get tired, They will walk and not become weary" (Is. 40:27-31).

Have I No Power to Deliver?

"Thus says the Lord, 'Where is the certificate of divorce By which I have sent your mother away? Or to whom of My creditors did I sell you? Behold, you were sold for your iniquities, And for your transgressions your mother was sent away. Why was there no man when I came? When I called, why was there none to answer? Is My hand so short that it cannot ransom? Or have I no power to deliver? Behold, I dry up the sea with My rebuke, I make the rivers a wilderness; Their fish stink for lack of water And die of thirst. I clothe the heavens with blackness And make sackcloth their covering'" (Is. 50:1-3).

IN THE BOOK OF JEREMIAH

He Made the Earth by His Power

"It is He who made the earth by His power, Who established the world by His wisdom; And by His understanding He has stretched out the heavens. When He utters His voice, there is a tumult of waters in the heavens, And He causes the clouds to ascend from the end of the earth; He makes lightning for the rain, And brings out the wind from His storehouses. Every man is stupid, devoid of knowledge; Every goldsmith is put to shame by his idols; For his molten images are deceitful, And there is no breath in them. They are worthless, a work of mockery; In the time of their punishment they will perish. The portion of Jacob is not like these; For the Maker of all is He, And Israel is the tribe of His inheritance; The Lord of hosts is His name" (Jer. 10:12-16).

I Will Make Them Know My Power and My Might

"Therefore behold, I am going to make them know — This time I will make them know My power and My might; And they shall know that My name is the Lord" (Jer. 16:21).

My Great Power and by My Outstretched Arm

"In the beginning of the reign of Zedekiah the son of Josiah, king of Judah, this word came to Jeremiah from the Lord, saying — thus says the Lord to me — Make for yourself bonds and yokes and put them on your neck, and send word to the king of Edom, to the king of Moab, to the king of the sons of Ammon, to the king of Tyre and to the king of Sidon by the messengers who come to Jerusalem to Zedekiah king of Judah. Command them to go to their masters, saying, 'Thus says the Lord of hosts, the God of Israel, thus you shall say to your masters, I have made the earth, the men and the beasts which are on the face of the earth by My great power and by My outstretched arm, and I will give it to the one who is pleasing in My sight. Now I have given all these lands into the hand of Nebuchadnezzar king of Babylon, My servant, and I have given him also the wild animals of the field to serve him. All the nations shall serve him and his son and his grandson until the time of his own land comes; then many nations and great kings will make him their servant'" (Jer. 27:1-7).

Heavens and the Earth by Your Great Power

"After I had given the deed of purchase to Baruch the son of Neriah, then I prayed to the Lord, saying, 'Ah Lord God! Behold, You have made the heavens and the earth by Your great power and by Your outstretched arm! Nothing is too difficult for You, who shows lovingkindness to thousands, but repays the iniquity of fathers into the bosom of their children after them, O great and mighty God. The Lord of hosts is His name; great in counsel and mighty in deed, whose eyes are open to all the ways of the sons of men, giving to everyone according to his ways and according to the fruit of his deeds; who has set signs and wonders in the land of Egypt, and even to this day both in Israel and among mankind; and You have made a name for Yourself, as at this day. You brought Your people Israel out of the land of Egypt with signs and with wonders, and with a strong hand and with an outstretched arm and with great terror; and gave them this land, which You swore to their forefathers to give them, a land flowing with milk and honey. They came in and took possession of it, but they did not obey Your voice or walk in Your law; they have done nothing of all that You commanded them to do; therefore You have made all this calamity come upon them. 'Behold, the siege ramps have reached the city to take it; and the city is given into the hand of the Chaldeans who fight against it, because of the sword, the famine and the pestilence; and what You have spoken has come to pass; and behold, You see it. You have said to me, O Lord God, "Buy for yourself the field with money and call in witnesses"—although the city is given into the hand of the Chaldeans"' (Jer. 32:16-25).

By His Power

"It is He who made the earth by His power, Who established the world by His wisdom, And by His understanding He stretched out the heavens. When He utters His voice, there is a tumult of waters in the heavens, And He causes the clouds to ascend from the end of the earth; He makes lightning for the rain And brings forth the wind from His storehouses. All mankind is stupid, devoid of knowledge; Every goldsmith is put to shame by his idols, For his molten images are deceitful, And there is no breath in them. They are worthless, a work of mockery; In the time of their punishment they will perish. The portion of Jacob is not like these; For the Maker of all is He, And of the tribe of His inheritance; The Lord of hosts is His name. He says, 'You are My war-club, My weapon of war; And with you I shatter nations, And with you I destroy kingdoms. With you I shatter the horse and his rider, And with you I shatter the chariot and its rider, And with you I shatter man and woman, And with you I shatter old man and youth, And with you I shatter young man and virgin, And with you I shatter the shepherd and his flock, And with you I shatter the farmer and his team, And with you I shatter governors and prefects'" (Jer. 51:15-23).

Chapter Two

IN THE BOOK OF DANIEL

Wisdom and Power Belong to Him

"Then the mystery was revealed to Daniel in a night vision. Then Daniel blessed the God of heaven; Daniel said, 'Let the name of God be blessed forever and ever, For wisdom and power belong to Him. It is He who changes the times and the epochs; He removes kings and establishes kings; He gives wisdom to wise men And knowledge to men of understanding. It is He who reveals the profound and hidden things; He knows what is in the darkness, And the light dwells with Him. To You, O God of my fathers, I give thanks and praise, For You have given me wisdom and power; Even now You have made known to me what we requested of You, For You have made known to us the king's matter'" (Da 2:19-23).

The Kingdom, the Power, the Strength and the Glory

"This was the dream; now we will tell its interpretation before the king. You, O king, are the king of kings, to whom the God of heaven has given the kingdom, the power, the strength and the glory; and wherever the sons of men dwell, or the beasts of the field, or the birds of the sky, He has given them into your hand and has caused you to rule over them all. You are the head of gold. After you there will arise another kingdom inferior to you, then another third kingdom of bronze, which will rule over all the earth. Then there will be a fourth kingdom as strong as iron; inasmuch as iron crushes and shatters all things, so, like iron that breaks in pieces, it will crush and break all these in pieces. In that you saw the feet and toes, partly of potter's clay and partly of iron, it will be a divided kingdom; but it will have in it the toughness of iron, inasmuch as you saw the iron mixed with common clay. As the toes of the feet were partly of iron and partly of pottery, so some of the kingdom will be strong and part of it will be brittle. And in that you saw the iron mixed with common clay, they will combine with one another in the seed of men; but they will not adhere to one another, even as iron does not combine with pottery. In the days of those kings the God of heaven will set up a kingdom which will never be destroyed, and that kingdom will not be left for another people; it will crush and put an end to all these kingdoms, but it will itself endure forever. Inasmuch as you saw that a stone was cut out of the mountain without hands and that it crushed the iron, the bronze, the clay, the silver and the gold, the great God has made known to the king what will take place in the future; so the dream is true and its interpretation is trustworthy" (Da. 2:36-45).

IN THE BOOK OF AMOS

I Will Even Unleash My Power upon Ekron

"Thus says the Lord, 'For three transgressions of Gaza and for four I will not revoke its punishment, Because they deported an entire population To deliver it up to Edom. So I will send fire upon the wall of Gaza And it will consume her citadels. I will also cut off the inhabitant from Ashdod, And him who holds the scepter, from Ashkelon; I will even unleash My power upon Ekron, And the remnant of the Philistines will perish,' Says the Lord God" (Am. 1:6-8).

IN THE BOOK OF MICAH

On the Other Hand I Am Filled with Power

"Thus says the Lord concerning the prophets Who lead my people astray; When they have something to bite with their teeth, They cry, 'Peace,' But against him who puts nothing in their mouths They declare holy war. Therefore it will be night for you—without vision, And darkness for you—without divination. The sun will go down on the prophets, And the day will become dark over them. The seers will be ashamed And the diviners will be embarrassed. Indeed, they will all cover their mouths Because there is no answer from God. On the other hand I am filled with power—With the Spirit of the Lord—And with justice and courage To make known to Jacob his rebellious act, Even to Israel his sin. Now hear this, heads of the house of Jacob And rulers of the house of Israel, Who abhor justice And twist everything that is straight, Who build Zion with bloodshed And Jerusalem with violent injustice. Her leaders pronounce judgment for a bribe, Her priests instruct for a price And her prophets divine for money. Yet they lean on the Lord saying, 'Is not the Lord in our midst? Calamity will not come upon us.' Therefore, on account of you

Zion will be plowed as a field, Jerusalem will become a heap of ruins, And the mountain of the temple will become high places of a forest" (Mic. 3:5-12).

IN THE BOOK OF NAHUM

Slow to Anger and Great in Power

"A jealous and avenging God is the Lord; The Lord is avenging and wrathful. The Lord takes vengeance on His adversaries, And He reserves wrath for His enemies. The Lord is slow to anger and great in power, And the Lord will by no means leave the guilty unpunished. In whirlwind and storm is His way, And clouds are the dust beneath His feet. He rebukes the sea and makes it dry; He dries up all the rivers. Bashan and Carmel wither; The blossoms of Lebanon wither. Mountains quake because of Him And the hills dissolve; Indeed the earth is upheaved by His presence, The world and all the inhabitants in it. Who can stand before His indignation? Who can endure the burning of His anger? His wrath is poured out like fire And the rocks are broken up by Him. The Lord is good, A stronghold in the day of trouble, And He knows those who take refuge in Him. But with an overflowing flood He will make a complete end of its site, And will pursue His enemies into darkness" (Na. 1:2-8).

IN THE BOOK OF HABAKKUK

There Is the Hiding of His Power

"God comes from Teman, And the Holy One from Mount Paran. Selah. His splendor covers the heavens, And the earth is full of His praise. His radiance is like the sunlight; He has rays flashing from His hand, And there is the hiding of His power. Before Him goes pestilence, And plague comes after Him. He stood and surveyed the earth; He looked and startled the nations. Yes, the perpetual mountains were shattered, The ancient hills collapsed. His ways are everlasting. I saw the tents of Cushan under distress, The tent curtains of the land of Midian were trembling" (Hab. 3:3-7).

Chapter Three

HIS POWER IN THE NEW TESTAMENT

IN THE BOOK OF MATTHEW

The Kingdom and the Power and the Glory Forever

"Pray, then, in this way: 'Our Father who is in heaven, Hallowed be Your name. Your kingdom come. Your will be done, On earth as it is in heaven. Give us this day our daily bread. And forgive us our debts, as we also have forgiven our debtors. And do not lead us into temptation, but deliver us from evil. For Yours is the kingdom and the power and the glory forever. Amen.' For if you forgive others for their transgressions, your heavenly Father will also forgive you. But if you do not forgive others, then your Father will not forgive your transgressions" (Mt. 6:9-15).

Not Understanding the Scriptures nor the Power of God

"But Jesus answered and said to them, 'You are mistaken, not understanding the Scriptures nor the power of God. For in the resurrection they neither marry nor are given in marriage, but are like angels in heaven. But regarding the resurrection of the dead, have you not read what was spoken to you by God: "I AM THE GOD OF ABRAHAM, AND THE GOD OF ISAAC, AND THE GOD OF JACOB"? He is not the God of the dead but of the living.' When the crowds heard this, they were astonished at His teaching" (Mt. 22:29-33).

Chapter Three

With Power and Great Glory

"But immediately after the tribulation of those days THE SUN WILL BE DARKENED, AND THE MOON WILL NOT GIVE ITS LIGHT, AND THE STARS WILL FALL from the sky, and the powers of the heavens will be shaken. And then the sign of the Son of Man will appear in the sky, and then all the tribes of the earth will mourn, and they will see the SON OF MAN COMING ON THE CLOUDS OF THE SKY with power and great glory. And He will send forth His angels with A GREAT TRUMPET and THEY WILL GATHER TOGETHER His elect from the four winds, from one end of the sky to the other" (Mt. 24:29-31).

At the Right Hand of Power

"Now the chief priests and the whole Council kept trying to obtain false testimony against Jesus, so that they might put Him to death. They did not find any, even though many false witnesses came forward. But later on two came forward, and said, 'This man stated, "I am able to destroy the temple of God and to rebuild it in three days."' The high priest stood up and said to Him, 'Do You not answer? What is it that these men are testifying against You?' But Jesus kept silent. And the high priest said to Him, "I adjure You by the living God, that You tell us whether You are the Christ, the Son of God.' Jesus said to him, 'You have said it yourself; nevertheless I tell you, hereafter you will see THE SON OF MAN SITTING AT THE RIGHT HAND OF POWER, and COMING ON THE CLOUDS OF HEAVEN'" (Mt. 26:59-64).

Chapter Three

IN THE BOOK OF MARK

The Power Proceeding from Him Had Gone Forth

"A woman who had had a hemorrhage for twelve years, and had endured much at the hands of many physicians, and had spent all that she had and was not helped at all, but rather had grown worse—after hearing about Jesus, she came up in the crowd behind Him and touched His cloak. For she thought, 'If I just touch His garments, I will get well.' Immediately the flow of her blood was dried up; and she felt in her body that she was healed of her affliction. Immediately Jesus, perceiving in Himself that the power proceeding from Him had gone forth, turned around in the crowd and said, 'Who touched My garments?' And His disciples said to Him, 'You see the crowd pressing in on You, and You say, "Who touched Me?"' And He looked around to see the woman who had done this. But the woman fearing and trembling, aware of what had happened to her, came and fell down before Him and told Him the whole truth. And He said to her, 'Daughter, your faith has made you well; go in peace and be healed of your affliction'" (Mk. 5:25-34).

The Kingdom of God After It Has Come with Power

"And Jesus was saying to them, 'Truly I say to you, there are some of those who are standing here who will not taste death until they see the kingdom of God after it has come with power'" (Mk. 9:1).

The Scriptures or the Power of God

"Some Sadducees (who say that there is no resurrection) came to Jesus, and began questioning Him, saying, 'Teacher, Moses wrote for us that IF A MAN'S BROTHER DIES and leaves behind a wife AND LEAVES NO CHILD, HIS BROTHER SHOULD MARRY THE WIFE AND RAISE UP CHILDREN TO HIS BROTHER. There were seven brothers; and the first took a wife, and died leaving no children. The second one married her, and died leaving behind no children; and the third likewise; and so all seven left no children. Last of all the woman died also. In the resurrection, when they rise again, which one's wife will she be? For all seven had married her.' Jesus said to them, 'Is this not the reason you are mistaken, that you do not understand the Scriptures or the power of God? For when they rise from the dead, they neither marry nor are given in marriage, but are like angels in heaven. But regarding the fact that the dead rise again, have you not read in the book of Moses, in the passage about the burning bush, how God spoke to him, saying, "I AM THE GOD OF ABRAHAM, AND THE GOD OF ISAAC, and the God of Jacob"? He is not the God of the dead, but of the living; you are greatly mistaken'" (Mk. 12:18-27).

Coming in Clouds with Great Power and Glory

"But in those days, after that tribulation, THE SUN WILL BE DARKENED AND THE MOON WILL NOT GIVE ITS LIGHT, AND THE STARS WILL BE FALLING from heaven, and the powers that are in the heavens will be shaken. Then they will see THE SON

OF MAN COMING IN CLOUDS with great power and glory. And then He will send forth the angels, and will gather together His elect from the four winds, from the farthest end of the earth to the farthest end of heaven" (Mk. 13:24-27).

Power, and Coming with the Clouds

"They led Jesus away to the high priest; and all the chief priests and the elders and the scribes gathered together. Peter had followed Him at a distance, right into the courtyard of the high priest; and he was sitting with the officers and warming himself at the fire. Now the chief priests and the whole Council kept trying to obtain testimony against Jesus to put Him to death, and they were not finding any. For many were giving false testimony against Him, but their testimony was not consistent. Some stood up and began to give false testimony against Him, saying, 'We heard Him say, "I will destroy this temple made with hands, and in three days I will build another made without hands."' Not even in this respect was their testimony consistent. The high priest stood up and came forward and questioned Jesus, saying, 'Do You not answer? What is it that these men are testifying against You?' But He kept silent and did not answer. Again the high priest was questioning Him, and saying to Him, 'Are You the Christ, the Son of the Blessed One?' And Jesus said, 'I am; and you shall see THE SON OF MAN SITTING AT THE RIGHT HAND OF POWER, and COMING WITH THE CLOUDS OF HEAVEN.' Tearing his clothes, the high priest said, 'What further need do we have of witnesses? You have heard the blasphemy; how does it seem to you?' And they all condemned Him to be deserving of death. Some began to spit at Him, and to blindfold Him, and to beat Him with their fists, and to say to Him, 'Prophesy!' And the officers received Him with slaps in the face" (Mk. 14:53-65).

IN THE BOOK OF LUKE

The Power of the Most High Will Overshadow You

"Now in the sixth month the angel Gabriel was sent from God to a city in Galilee called Nazareth, to a virgin engaged to a man whose name was Joseph, of the descendants of David; and the virgin's name was Mary. And coming in, he said to her, 'Greetings, favored one! The Lord is with you.' But she was very perplexed at this statement, and kept pondering what kind of salutation this was. The angel said to her, 'Do not be afraid, Mary; for you have found favor with God. And behold, you will conceive in your womb and bear a son, and you shall name Him Jesus. He will be great and will be called the Son of the Most High; and the Lord God will give Him the throne of His father David; and He will reign over the house of Jacob forever, and His kingdom will have no end.' Mary said to the angel, 'How can this be, since I am a virgin?' The angel answered and said to her, 'The Holy Spirit will come upon you, and the power of the Most High will overshadow you; and for that reason the holy Child shall be called the Son of God. And behold, even your relative Elizabeth has also conceived a son in her old age; and she who was called barren is now in her sixth month. For nothing will be impossible with God.' And Mary said, 'Behold, the bondslave of the Lord; may it be done to me according to your word.' And the angel departed from her" (Lk. 1:26-38).

In the Power of the Spirit, and News Spread

"And Jesus returned to Galilee in the power of the Spirit, and news about Him spread through all the surrounding district. And He began teaching in their synagogues and was praised by all" (Lk. 4:14-15).

For with Authority and Power He Commands

"And He came down to Capernaum, a city of Galilee, and He was teaching them on the Sabbath; and they were amazed at His teaching, for His message was with authority. In the synagogue there was a man possessed by the spirit of an unclean demon, and he cried out with a loud voice, 'Let us alone! What business do we have with each other, Jesus of Nazareth? Have You come to destroy us? I know who You are—the Holy One of God!' But Jesus rebuked him, saying, 'Be quiet and come out of him!' And when the demon had thrown him down in the midst of the people, he came out of him without doing him any harm. And amazement came upon them all, and they began talking with one another saying, 'What is this message? For with authority and power He commands the unclean spirits and they come out.' And the report about Him was spreading into every locality in the surrounding district" (Lk. 4:31-37).

The Power of the Lord Was Present

"One day He was teaching; and there were some Pharisees and teachers of the law sitting there, who had come from every village of Galilee and Judea and from Jerusalem; and the power of the Lord was present for Him to perform healing. And some men were carrying on a bed a man who was paralyzed; and they were trying to bring him in and to set him down in front of Him. But not finding any way to bring him in because of the crowd, they went up on the roof and let him down through the tiles with his stretcher, into the middle of the crowd, in front of Jesus. Seeing their faith, He said, 'Friend, your sins are forgiven you.' The scribes and the Pharisees began to reason, saying, 'Who is this man who speaks blasphemies? Who can forgive sins, but God alone?' But Jesus, aware of their reasonings, answered and said to them, 'Why are you reasoning in your hearts? Which is easier, to say, "Your sins have been forgiven you," or to say, "Get up and walk"? But, so that you may know that the Son of Man has authority on earth to forgive sins,'—He said to the paralytic—'I say to you, get up, and pick up your stretcher and go home.' Immediately he got up before them, and picked up what he had been lying on, and went home glorifying God. They were all struck with astonishment and began glorifying God; and they were filled with fear, saying, 'We have seen remarkable things today'" (Lk. 5:17-26).

Power Was Coming from Him and Healing them All

"Jesus came down with them and stood on a level place; and there was a large crowd of His disciples, and a great throng of people from all Judea and Jerusalem and the coastal region of Tyre and Sidon, who had come to hear Him and to be healed of their diseases;

and those who were troubled with unclean spirits were being cured. And all the people were trying to touch Him, for power was coming from Him and healing them all" (Lk. 6:17-19).

I Was Aware that Power Had Gone Out of Me

"And a woman who had a hemorrhage for twelve years, and could not be healed by anyone, came up behind Him and touched the fringe of His cloak, and immediately her hemorrhage stopped. And Jesus said, 'Who is the one who touched Me?' And while they were all denying it, Peter said, 'Master, the people are crowding and pressing in on You.' But Jesus said, 'Someone did touch Me, for I was aware that power had gone out of Me.' When the woman saw that she had not escaped notice, she came trembling and fell down before Him, and declared in the presence of all the people the reason why she had touched Him, and how she had been immediately healed. And He said to her, 'Daughter, your faith has made you well; go in peace'" (Lk. 8:43-48).

Power and Authority Over All the Demons

"And He called the twelve together, and gave them power and authority over all the demons and to heal diseases. And He sent them out to proclaim the kingdom of God and to perform healing. And He said to them, 'Take nothing for your journey, neither a staff, nor a bag, nor bread, nor money; and do not even have two tunics apiece. Whatever house you enter, stay there until you leave that city. And as for those who do not receive you, as you go out from that city, shake the dust off your feet as a testimony against them.' Departing, they began going throughout the villages, preaching the gospel and healing everywhere" (Lk. 9:1-6).

Over All the Power of the Enemy

"The seventy returned with joy, saying, 'Lord, even the demons are subject to us in Your name.' And He said to them, 'I was watching Satan fall from heaven like lightning. Behold, I have given you authority to tread on serpents and scorpions, and over all the power of the enemy, and nothing will injure you. Nevertheless do not rejoice in this, that the spirits are subject to you, but rejoice that your names are recorded in heaven'" (Lk. 10:17-20).

On a Cloud with Power and Great Glory

"There will be signs in sun and moon and stars, and on the earth dismay among nations, in perplexity at the roaring of the sea and the waves, men fainting from fear and the expectation of the things which are coming upon the world; for the powers of the heavens will be shaken. Then they will see THE SON OF MAN COMING IN A CLOUD with power and great glory. But when these things begin to take place, straighten up and lift up your heads, because your redemption is drawing near" (Lk. 21:25-28).

At the Right Hand of the Power of God

"When it was day, the Council of elders of the people assembled, both chief priests and scribes, and they led Him away to their council chamber, saying, 'If

You are the Christ, tell us.' But He said to them, 'If I tell you, you will not believe; and if I ask a question, you will not answer. But from now on THE SON OF MAN WILL BE SEATED AT THE RIGHT HAND of the power OF GOD.' And they all said, 'Are You the Son of God, then?' And He said to them, 'Yes, I am.' Then they said, 'What further need do we have of testimony? For we have heard it ourselves from His own mouth'" (Lk. 22:66-71).

Until You Are Clothed with Power from on High

"Now He said to them, 'These are My words which I spoke to you while I was still with you, that all things which are written about Me in the Law of Moses and the Prophets and the Psalms must be fulfilled.' Then He opened their minds to understand the Scriptures, and He said to them, 'Thus it is written, that the Christ would suffer and rise again from the dead the third day, and that repentance for forgiveness of sins would be proclaimed in His name to all the nations, beginning from Jerusalem. You are witnesses of these things. And behold, I am sending forth the promise of My Father upon you; but you are to stay in the city until you are clothed with power from on high'" (Lk. 24:44-49).

IN THE BOOK OF ACTS

You Will Receive Power When the Holy Spirit Has Come upon You

"So when they had come together, they were asking Him, saying, 'Lord, is it at this time You are restoring the kingdom to Israel?' He said to them, 'It is not for you to know times or epochs which the Father has fixed by His own authority; but you will receive power when the Holy Spirit has come upon you; and you shall be My witnesses both in Jerusalem, and in all Judea and Samaria, and even to the remotest part of the earth.' And after He had said these things, He was lifted up while they were looking on, and a cloud received Him out of their sight. And as they were gazing intently into the sky while He was going, behold, two men in white clothing stood beside them. They also said, 'Men of Galilee, why do you stand looking into the sky? This Jesus, who has been taken up from you into heaven, will come in just the same way as you have watched Him go into heaven'" (Ac. 1:6-11).

As if by Our Own Power or Piety

"While he was clinging to Peter and John, all the people ran together to them at the so-called portico of Solomon, full of amazement. But when Peter saw this, he replied to the people, 'Men of Israel, why are you amazed at this, or why do you gaze at us, as if by our own power or piety we had made him walk? The God of Abraham, Isaac and Jacob, the God of our fathers, has glorified His servant Jesus, the one whom you delivered and disowned in the presence of Pilate, when he had decided to release Him. But you disowned the Holy and Righteous One and asked for a murderer to be granted to you, but put to death the Prince of life, the one whom God raised from the dead, a fact to which we are witnesses. And on the basis of faith in His name, it is the name of Jesus which has strengthened this man whom you see and know; and the faith which comes through

Him has given him this perfect health in the presence of you all'" (Ac. 3:11-16).

And with Great Power They Were Giving Testimony

"And the congregation of those who believed were of one heart and soul; and not one of them claimed that anything belonging to him was his own, but all things were common property to them. And with great power the apostles were giving testimony to the resurrection of the Lord Jesus, and abundant grace was upon them all. For there was not a needy person among them, for all who were owners of land or houses would sell them and bring the proceeds of the sales and lay them at the apostles' feet, and they would be distributed to each as any had need" (Ac. 4:32-35).

Full of Grace and Power, Was Performing Wonders

"And Stephen, full of grace and power, was performing great wonders and signs among the people. But some men from what was called the Synagogue of the Freedmen, including both Cyrenians and Alexandrians, and some from Cilicia and Asia, rose up and argued with Stephen. But they were unable to cope with the wisdom and the Spirit with which he was speaking. Then they secretly induced men to say, 'We have heard him speak blasphemous words against Moses and against God.' And they stirred up the people, the elders and the scribes, and they came up to him and dragged him away and brought him before the Council. They put forward false witnesses who said, 'This man incessantly speaks against this holy place and the Law; for we have heard him say that this Nazarene,

Jesus, will destroy this place and alter the customs which Moses handed down to us.' And fixing their gaze on him, all who were sitting in the Council saw his face like the face of an angel" (Ac. 6:8-15).

This Man Is What Is Called the Great Power of God

"Now there was a man named Simon, who formerly was practicing magic in the city and astonishing the people of Samaria, claiming to be someone great; and they all, from smallest to greatest, were giving attention to him, saying, 'This man is what is called the Great Power of God.' And they were giving him attention because he had for a long time astonished them with his magic arts. But when they believed Philip preaching the good news about the kingdom of God and the name of Jesus Christ, they were being baptized, men and women alike. Even Simon himself believed; and after being baptized, he continued on with Philip, and as he observed signs and great miracles taking place, he was constantly amazed" (Ac. 8:9-13).

With the Holy Spirit and with Power

"Opening his mouth, Peter said: 'I most certainly understand now that God is not one to show partiality, but in every nation the man who fears Him and does what is right is welcome to Him. The word which He sent to the sons of Israel, preaching peace through Jesus Christ (He is Lord of all)—you yourselves know the thing which took place throughout all Judea, starting from Galilee, after the baptism which John proclaimed. You know of Jesus of Nazareth, how God anointed Him with the Holy Spirit and with power, and how He went about doing good and healing all who were oppressed by the devil, for God was with Him. We are witnesses of all the things He did both in the land of the Jews and in Jerusalem. They also put Him to death by hanging Him on a cross. God raised Him up on the third day and granted that He become visible, not to all the people, but to witnesses who were chosen beforehand by God, that is, to us who ate and drank with Him after He arose from the dead. And He ordered us to preach to the people, and solemnly to testify that this is the One who has been appointed by God as Judge of the living and the dead. Of Him all the prophets bear witness that through His name everyone who believes in Him receives forgiveness of sins'" (Ac. 10:34-43).

IN THE BOOK OF ROMANS

With Power by the Resurrection from the Dead

"Paul, a bond-servant of Christ Jesus, called as an apostle, set apart for the gospel of God, which He promised beforehand through His prophets in the holy Scriptures, concerning His Son, who was born of a descendant of David according to the flesh, who was declared the Son of God with power by the resurrection from the dead, according to the Spirit of holiness, Jesus Christ our Lord, through whom we have received grace and apostleship to bring about the obedience of faith among all the Gentiles for His name's sake, among whom you also are the called of Jesus Christ; to all who are beloved of God in Rome, called as saints: Grace to you and peace from God our Father and the Lord Jesus Christ" (Ro. 1:1-7).

Chapter Three

It Is the Power of God for Salvation

"For I am not ashamed of the gospel, for it is the power of God for salvation to everyone who believes, to the Jew first and also to the Greek. For in it the righteousness of God is revealed from faith to faith; as it is written, 'BUT THE RIGHTEOUS man SHALL LIVE BY FAITH'" (Ro. 1:16-17).

His Attributes and Eternal Power Have Been Clearly Seen

"For the wrath of God is revealed from heaven against all ungodliness and unrighteousness of men who suppress the truth in unrighteousness, because that which is known about God is evident within them; for God made it evident to them. For since the creation of the world His invisible attributes, His eternal power and divine nature, have been clearly seen, being understood through what has been made, so that they are without excuse. For even though they knew God, they did not honor Him as God or give thanks, but they became futile in their speculations, and their foolish heart was darkened. Professing to be wise, they became fools, and exchanged the glory of the incorruptible God for an image in the form of corruptible man and of birds and four-footed animals and crawling creatures" (Ro. 1:18-23).

To Demonstrate My Power in You

"What shall we say then? There is no injustice with God, is there? May it never be! For He says to Moses, 'I WILL HAVE MERCY ON WHOM I HAVE

MERCY, AND I WILL HAVE COMPASSION ON WHOM I HAVE COMPASSION.' So then it does not depend on the man who wills or the man who runs, but on God who has mercy. For the Scripture says to Pharaoh, 'FOR THIS VERY PURPOSE I RAISED YOU UP, TO DEMONSTRATE MY POWER IN YOU, AND THAT MY NAME MIGHT BE PROCLAIMED THROUGHOUT THE WHOLE EARTH.' So then He has mercy on whom He desires, and He hardens whom He desires" (Ro. 9:14-18).

Demonstrate His Wrath and to Make His Power Known

"You will say to me then, 'Why does He still find fault? For who resists His will?" On the contrary, who are you, O man, who answers back to God? The thing molded will not say to the molder, 'Why did you make me like this," will it? Or does not the potter have a right over the clay, to make from the same lump one vessel for honorable use and another for common use? What if God, although willing to demonstrate His wrath and to make His power known, endured with much patience vessels of wrath prepared for destruction? And He did so to make known the riches of His glory upon vessels of mercy, which He prepared beforehand for glory, even us, whom He also called, not from among Jews only, but also from among Gentiles. As He says also in Hosea, 'I WILL CALL THOSE WHO WERE NOT MY PEOPLE, "MY PEOPLE," AND HER WHO WAS NOT BELOVED, "BELOVED." AND IT SHALL BE THAT IN THE PLACE WHERE IT WAS SAID TO THEM, "YOU ARE NOT MY PEOPLE," THERE THEY SHALL BE CALLED SONS OF THE LIVING GOD'" (Ro. 9:19-26).

Abound in Hope by the Power of the Holy Spirit.

"Again Isaiah says, 'THERE SHALL COME THE ROOT OF JESSE, AND HE WHO ARISES TO RULE OVER THE GENTILES, IN HIM SHALL THE GENTILES HOPE.' Now may the God of hope fill you with all joy and peace in believing, so that you will abound in hope by the power of the Holy Spirit" (Ro. 15:12-13).

The Power of Signs and Wonders

"And concerning you, my brethren, I myself also am convinced that you yourselves are full of goodness, filled with all knowledge and able also to admonish one another. But I have written very boldly to you on some points so as to remind you again, because of the grace that was given me from God, to be a minister of Christ Jesus to the Gentiles, ministering as a priest the gospel of God, so that my offering of the Gentiles may become acceptable, sanctified by the Holy Spirit. Therefore in Christ Jesus I have found reason for boasting in things pertaining to God. For I will not presume to speak of anything except what Christ has accomplished through me, resulting in the obedience of the Gentiles by word and deed, in the power of signs and wonders, in the power of the Spirit; so that from Jerusalem and round about as far as Illyricum I have fully preached the gospel of Christ. And thus I aspired to preach the gospel, not where Christ was already named, so that I would not build on another man's foundation; but as it is written, 'THEY WHO HAD NO NEWS OF HIM SHALL SEE, AND THEY WHO HAVE NOT HEARD SHALL UNDERSTAND'" (Ro. 15:14-21).

Chapter Three

IN THE BOOK OF 1 CORINTHIANS

Christ the Power of God and the Wisdom of God

"For the word of the cross is foolishness to those who are perishing, but to us who are being saved it is the power of God. For it is written, 'I WILL DESTROY THE WISDOM OF THE WISE, AND THE CLEVERNESS OF THE CLEVER I WILL SET ASIDE.' Where is the wise man? Where is the scribe? Where is the debater of this age? Has not God made foolish the wisdom of the world? For since in the wisdom of God the world through its wisdom did not come to know God, God was well-pleased through the foolishness of the message preached to save those who believe. For indeed Jews ask for signs and Greeks search for wisdom; but we preach Christ crucified, to Jews a stumbling block and to Gentiles foolishness, but to those who are the called, both Jews and Greeks, Christ the power of God and the wisdom of God. Because the foolishness of God is wiser than men, and the weakness of God is stronger than men" (1Co. 1:18-25).

Preaching in Demonstration of the Spirit and of Power

"And when I came to you, brethren, I did not come with superiority of speech or of wisdom, proclaiming to you the testimony of God. For I determined to know nothing among you except Jesus Christ, and Him crucified. I was with you in weakness and in fear and in much trembling, and my message and my preaching were not in persuasive words of wisdom, but in demonstration of the Spirit and of power, so that your faith would not rest on the wisdom of men, but on the power of God" (1Co. 2:1-5).

Does Not Consist in Words but in Power

"I do not write these things to shame you, but to admonish you as my beloved children. For if you were to have countless tutors in Christ, yet you would not have many fathers, for in Christ Jesus I became your father through the gospel. Therefore I exhort you, be imitators of me. For this reason I have sent to you Timothy, who is my beloved and faithful child in the Lord, and he will remind you of my ways which are in Christ, just as I teach everywhere in every church. Now some have become arrogant, as though I were not coming to you. But I will come to you soon, if the Lord wills, and I shall find out, not the words of those who are arrogant but their power. For the kingdom of God does not consist in words but in power. What do you desire? Shall I come to you with a rod, or with love and a spirit of gentleness" (1Co. 4:14-21)?

The Power of Our Lord Jesus

"For I, on my part, though absent in body but present in spirit, have already judged him who has so committed this, as though I were present. In the name of our Lord Jesus, when you are assembled, and I with you in spirit, with the power of our Lord Jesus, I have decided to deliver such a one to Satan for the destruction of his flesh, so that his spirit may be saved in the day of the Lord Jesus" (1Co. 5:3-5).

Will Also Raise Us up Through His Power

"All things are lawful for me, but not all things are profitable. All things are lawful for me, but I will not be mastered by anything. Food is for the stomach and the stomach is for food, but God will do away with both of them. Yet the body is not for immorality, but for the Lord, and the Lord is for the body. Now God has not only raised the Lord, but will also raise us up through His power. Do you not know that your bodies are members of Christ? Shall I then take away the members of Christ and make them members of a prostitute? May it never be! Or do you not know that the one who joins himself to a prostitute is one body with her? For He says, 'THE TWO SHALL BECOME ONE FLESH.' But the one who joins himself to the Lord is one spirit with Him. Flee immorality. Every other sin that a man commits is outside the body, but the immoral man sins against his own body. Or do you not know that your body is a temple of the Holy Spirit who is in you, whom you have from God, and that you are not your own? For you have been bought with a price: therefore glorify God in your body" (1Co. 6:12-20).

He Has Abolished All Rule and All Authority and Power

"But now Christ has been raised from the dead, the first fruits of those who are asleep. For since by a man came death, by a man also came the resurrection of the dead. For as in Adam all die, so also in Christ all will be made alive. But each in his own order: Christ the first fruits, after that those who are Christ's at His coming, then comes the end, when He hands over the kingdom to the God and Father, when He has abolished all rule and all authority and power. For He must reign until He has put all His enemies under His feet. The last enemy that will be abolished is death. For HE HAS PUT ALL THINGS IN SUBJECTION UNDER HIS FEET. But when He says, 'All things are put in subjection,' it is evident that He is excepted who put all things in subjection to Him. When all things are subjected to Him, then the Son Himself also will be subjected to the One who subjected all things to Him, so that God may be all in all" (1Co. 15:20-28).

It Is Sown in Weakness, It Is Raised in Power

"So also is the resurrection of the dead. It is sown a perishable body, it is raised an imperishable body; it is sown in dishonor, it is raised in glory; it is sown in weakness, it is raised in power; it is sown a natural body, it is raised a spiritual body. If there is a natural body, there is also a spiritual body. So also it is written, 'The first MAN, Adam, BECAME A LIVING SOUL.' The last Adam became a life-giving spirit. However, the spiritual is not first, but the natural; then the spiritual. The first man is from the earth, earthy; the second man is from heaven. As is the earthy, so also are those who are earthy; and as is the heavenly, so also are those who are heavenly. Just as we have borne the image of the earthy, we will also bear the image of the heavenly" (1Co. 15:42-49).

IN THE BOOK OF 2 CORINTHIANS

Chapter Three

The Power Will Be of God

"But we have this treasure in earthen vessels, so that the surpassing greatness of the power will be of God and not from ourselves; we are afflicted in every way, but not crushed; perplexed, but not despairing; persecuted, but not forsaken; struck down, but not destroyed; always carrying about in the body the dying of Jesus, so that the life of Jesus also may be manifested in our body. For we who live are constantly being delivered over to death for Jesus' sake, so that the life of Jesus also may be manifested in our mortal flesh. So death works in us, but life in you" (2Co. 4:7-12).

The Power of God; by the Weapons of Righteousness

"And working together with Him, we also urge you not to receive the grace of God in vain — for He says, 'AT THE ACCEPTABLE TIME I LISTENED TO YOU, AND ON THE DAY OF SALVATION I HELPED YOU.' Behold, now is 'THE ACCEPTABLE TIME,' behold, now is 'THE DAY OF SALVATION' — giving no cause for offense in anything, so that the ministry will not be discredited, but in everything commending ourselves as servants of God, in much endurance, in afflictions, in hardships, in distresses, in beatings, in imprisonments, in tumults, in labors, in sleeplessness, in hunger, in purity, in knowledge, in patience, in kindness, in the Holy Spirit, in genuine love, in the word of truth, in the power of God; by the weapons of righteousness for the right hand and the left, by glory and dishonor, by evil report and good report; regarded as deceivers and yet true; as unknown yet well-known, as dying yet behold, we live; as punished yet not put to death, as sorrowful yet always rejoicing, as poor yet making many rich, as having nothing yet possessing all things" (2Co. 6:1-10).

Power Is Perfected in Weakness

"Boasting is necessary, though it is not profitable; but I will go on to visions and revelations of the Lord. I know a man in Christ who fourteen years ago—whether in the body I do not know, or out of the body I do not know, God knows—such a man was caught up to the third heaven. And I know how such a man—whether in the body or apart from the body I do not know, God knows— was caught up into Paradise and heard inexpressible words, which a man is not permitted to speak. On behalf of such a man I will boast; but on my own behalf I will not boast, except in regard to my weaknesses. For if I do wish to boast I will not be foolish, for I will be speaking the truth; but I refrain from this, so that no one will credit me with more than he sees in me or hears from me. Because of the surpassing greatness of the revelations, for this reason, to keep me from exalting myself, there was given me a thorn in the flesh, a messenger of Satan to torment me— to keep me from exalting myself! Concerning this I implored the Lord three times that it might leave me. And He has said to me, 'My grace is sufficient for you, for power is perfected in weakness.' Most gladly, therefore, I will rather boast about my weaknesses, so that the power of Christ may dwell in me. Therefore I am well content with weaknesses, with insults, with distresses, with persecutions, with difficulties, for Christ's sake; for when I am weak, then I am strong" (2Co. 12:1-10).

Chapter Three

He Lives Because of the Power of God

"This is the third time I am coming to you. EVERY FACT IS TO BE CONFIRMED BY THE TESTIMONY OF TWO OR THREE WITNESSES. I have previously said when present the second time, and though now absent I say in advance to those who have sinned in the past and to all the rest as well, that if I come again I will not spare anyone, since you are seeking for proof of the Christ who speaks in me, and who is not weak toward you, but mighty in you. For indeed He was crucified because of weakness, yet He lives because of the power of God. For we also are weak in Him, yet we will live with Him because of the power of God directed toward you" (2Co. 13:1-4).

IN THE BOOK OF EPHESIANS

Far Above All Rule and Authority and Power

"For this reason I too, having heard of the faith in the Lord Jesus which exists among you and your love for all the saints, do not cease giving thanks for you, while making mention of you in my prayers; that the God of our Lord Jesus Christ, the Father of glory, may give to you a spirit of wisdom and of revelation in the knowledge of Him. I pray that the eyes of your heart may be enlightened, so that you will know what is the hope of His calling, what are the riches of the glory of His inheritance in the saints, and what is the surpassing greatness of His power toward us who believe. These are in accordance with the working of the strength of His might which He brought about in Christ, when He raised Him from the dead and seated Him at His right hand in the heavenly places, far above all rule and authority and power and dominion, and every name that is named, not only in this age but also in the one to come. And He put all things in subjection under His feet, and gave Him as head over all things to the church, which is His body, the fullness of Him who fills all in all" (Eph. 1:15-23).

Me According to the Working of His Power

"For this reason I, Paul, the prisoner of Christ Jesus for the sake of you Gentiles—if indeed you have heard of the stewardship of God's grace which was given to me for you; that by revelation there was made known to me the mystery, as I wrote before in brief. By referring to this, when you read you can understand my insight into the mystery of Christ, which in other generations was not made known to the sons of men, as it has now been revealed to His holy apostles and prophets in the Spirit; to be specific, that the Gentiles are fellow heirs and fellow members of the body, and fellow partakers of the promise in Christ Jesus through the gospel, of which I was made a minister, according to the gift of God's grace which was given to me according to the working of His power. To me, the very least of all saints, this grace was given, to preach to the Gentiles the unfathomable riches of Christ, and to bring to light what is the administration of the mystery which for ages has been hidden in God who created all things; so that the manifold wisdom of God might now be made known through the church to the rulers and the authorities in the heavenly places. This was in accordance with the eternal purpose which He carried out in Christ Jesus our Lord, in whom we have boldness and confident access through faith in Him. Therefore I ask you not to lose heart at my tribulations on your behalf, for they are your glory" (Eph. 3:1-13).

Strengthened with Power Through His Spirit

"For this reason I bow my knees before the Father, from whom every family in heaven and on earth derives its name, that He would grant you, according to the riches of His glory, to be strengthened with power through His Spirit in the inner man, so that Christ may dwell in your hearts through faith; and that you, being rooted and grounded in love, may be able to comprehend with all the saints what is the breadth and length and height and depth, and to know the love of Christ which surpasses knowledge, that you may be filled up to all the fullness of God" (Eph. 3:14-19).

According to the Power that Works Within Us

"Now to Him who is able to do far more abundantly beyond all that we ask or think, according to the power that works within us, to Him be the glory in the church and in Christ Jesus to all generations forever and ever. Amen" (Eph. 3:20-21).

IN THE BOOK OF PHILIPPIANS

Know Him and the Power of His Resurrection

"But whatever things were gain to me, those things I have counted as loss for the sake of Christ. More than that, I count all things to be loss in view of the surpassing value of knowing Christ Jesus my Lord, for whom I have suffered the loss of all things, and count them but rubbish so that I may gain Christ, and may be found in Him, not having a righteousness of my own derived from the Law, but that which is through faith in Christ, the righteousness which comes from God on the basis of faith, that I may know Him and the power of His resurrection and the fellowship of His sufferings, being conformed to His death; in order that I may attain to the resurrection from the dead" (Php. 3:7-11).

The Exertion of the Power

"Brethren, join in following my example, and observe those who walk according to the pattern you have in us. For many walk, of whom I often told you, and now tell you even weeping, that they are enemies of the cross of Christ, whose end is destruction, whose god is their appetite, and whose glory is in their shame, who set their minds on earthly things. For our citizenship is in heaven, from which also we eagerly wait for a Savior, the Lord Jesus Christ; who will transform the body of our humble state into conformity with the body of His glory, by the exertion of the power that He has even to subject all things to Himself" (Php. 3:17-21).

IN THE BOOK OF COLOSSIANS

Strengthened with All Power

"For this reason also, since the day we heard of it, we have not ceased to pray for you and to ask that you may be filled with the knowledge of His will in all spiritual wisdom and understanding, so that you will walk in a manner worthy of the Lord, to please Him in all respects, bearing fruit in every good work and increasing in the knowledge of God; strengthened with all power, according to His glorious might, for the attaining of all steadfastness and patience; joyously giving thanks to the Father, who has qualified us to share in the inheritance of the saints in Light. For He rescued us from the domain of darkness, and transferred us to the kingdom of His beloved Son, in whom we have redemption, the forgiveness of sins" (Col. 1:9-14).

His Power, Which Mightily Works Within Me

"Now I rejoice in my sufferings for your sake, and in my flesh I do my share on behalf of His body, which is the church, in filling up what is lacking in Christ's afflictions. Of this church I was made a minister according to the stewardship from God bestowed on me for your benefit, so that I might fully carry out the preaching of the word of God, that is, the mystery which has been hidden from the past ages and generations, but has now been manifested to His saints, to whom God willed to make known what is the riches of the glory of this mystery among the Gentiles, which is Christ in you, the hope of glory. We proclaim Him, admonishing every man and teaching every man with all wisdom, so that we may present every man complete in Christ. For this purpose also I labor, striving according to His power, which mightily works within me" (Col. 1:24-29).

IN THE BOOK OF 1 THESSALONIANS

Chapter Three

In Power and in the Holy Spirit and with Full Conviction

"We give thanks to God always for all of you, making mention of you in our prayers; constantly bearing in mind your work of faith and labor of love and steadfastness of hope in our Lord Jesus Christ in the presence of our God and Father, knowing, brethren beloved by God, His choice of you; for our gospel did not come to you in word only, but also in power and in the Holy Spirit and with full conviction; just as you know what kind of men we proved to be among you for your sake. You also became imitators of us and of the Lord, having received the word in much tribulation with the joy of the Holy Spirit, so that you became an example to all the believers in Macedonia and in Achaia. For the word of the Lord has sounded forth from you, not only in Macedonia and Achaia, but also in every place your faith toward God has gone forth, so that we have no need to say anything. For they themselves report about us what kind of a reception we had with you, and how you turned to God from idols to serve a living and true God, and to wait for His Son from heaven, whom He raised from the dead, that is Jesus, who rescues us from the wrath to come" (1Th. 1:2-10).

IN THE BOOK OF 2 THESSALONIANS

Away from the Glory of His Power

"We ought always to give thanks to God for you, brethren, as is only fitting, because your faith is greatly enlarged, and the love of each one of you toward one another grows ever greater; therefore, we ourselves speak proudly of you among the churches of God for your perseverance and faith in the midst of all your persecutions and afflictions which you endure. This is a plain indication of God's righteous judgment so that you will be considered worthy of the kingdom of God, for which indeed you are suffering. For after all it is only just for God to repay with affliction those who afflict you, and to give relief to you who are afflicted and to us as well when the Lord Jesus will be revealed from heaven with His mighty angels in flaming fire, dealing out retribution to those who do not know God and to those who do not obey the gospel of our Lord Jesus. These will pay the penalty of eternal destruction, away from the presence of the Lord and from the glory of His power, when He comes to be glorified in His saints on that day, and to be marveled at among all who have believed—for our testimony to you was believed. To this end also we pray for you always, that our God will count you worthy of your calling, and fulfill every desire for goodness and the work of faith with power, so that the name of our Lord Jesus will be glorified in you, and you in Him, according to the grace of our God and the Lord Jesus Christ" (2Th. 1:3-12).

IN THE BOOK OF 2 TIMOTHY

But of Power and Love and Discipline

"I thank God, whom I serve with a clear conscience the way my forefathers did, as I constantly remember you in my prayers night and day, longing to see you, even as I recall your tears, so that I may be filled with joy. For I am mindful of the sincere faith within you, which first dwelt in your grandmother Lois and your mother Eunice, and I am sure that it is in you as well. For this reason I remind you to kindle afresh the gift of God which is in you through the laying on of my hands. For God has not given us a spirit of timidity, but of power and love and discipline" (2Ti. 1:3-7).

Suffering for the Gospel According to the Power of God

"Therefore do not be ashamed of the testimony of our Lord or of me His prisoner, but join with me in suffering for the gospel according to the power of God, who has saved us and called us with a holy calling, not according to our works, but according to His own purpose and grace which was granted us in Christ Jesus from all eternity, but now has been revealed by the appearing of our Savior Christ Jesus, who abolished death and brought life and immortality to light through the gospel, for which I was appointed a preacher and an apostle and a teacher. For this reason I also suffer these things, but I am not ashamed; for I know whom I have believed and I am convinced that He is able to guard what I have entrusted to Him until that day. Retain the standard of sound words which you have heard from me, in the faith and love which are in Christ Jesus. Guard, through the Holy Spirit who dwells in us, the treasure which has been entrusted to you" (2Ti. 1:8-14).

They Denied Its Power; Avoid Such Men as These

"But realize this, that in the last days difficult times will come. For men will be lovers of self, lovers of money, boastful, arrogant, revilers, disobedient to parents, ungrateful, unholy, unloving, irreconcilable, malicious gossips, without self-control, brutal, haters of good, treacherous, reckless, conceited, lovers of pleasure rather than lovers of God, holding to a form of godliness, although they have denied its power; Avoid such men as these. For among them are those who enter into households and captivate weak women weighed down with sins, led on by various impulses, always learning and never able to come to the knowledge of the truth. Just as Jannes and Jambres opposed Moses, so these men also oppose the truth, men of depraved mind, rejected in regard to the faith. But they will not make further progress; for their folly will be obvious to all, just as Jannes's and Jambres's folly was also" (2Ti. 3:1-9).

IN THE BOOK OF HEBREWS

All Things by the Word of His Power

"God, after He spoke long ago to the fathers in the prophets in many portions and in many ways, in these last days has spoken to us in His Son, whom He appointed heir of all things, through whom also He made the world. And He is the radiance of His glory and the exact representation of His nature, and upholds all things by the word of His power. When He had made purification of sins, He sat down at the right hand of the Majesty on high, having become as much better than the angels, as He has inherited a more excellent name than they" (Heb. 1:1-4).

Render Powerless Him Who Had the Power of Death

"Therefore, since the children share in flesh and blood, He Himself likewise also partook of the same, that through death He might render powerless him who had the power of death, that is, the devil, and might free those who through fear of death were subject to slavery all their lives. For assuredly He does not give help to angels, but He gives help to the descendant of Abraham. Therefore, He had to be made like His brethren in all things, so that He might become a merciful and faithful high priest in things pertaining to God, to make propitiation for the sins of the people. For since He Himself was tempted in that which He has suffered, He is able to come to the aid of those who are tempted" (Heb. 2:14-18).

IN THE BOOK OF 1 PETER

Protected by the Power of God Through Faith

"Blessed be the God and Father of our Lord Jesus Christ, who according to His great mercy has caused us to be born again to a living hope through the resurrection of Jesus Christ from the dead, to obtain an inheritance which is imperishable and undefiled and will not fade away, reserved in heaven for you, who are protected by the power of God through faith for a salvation ready to be revealed in the last time. In this you greatly rejoice, even though now for a little while, if necessary, you have been distressed by various trials, so that the proof of your faith, being more precious than gold which is perishable, even though tested by fire, may be found to result in praise and glory and honor at the revelation of Jesus Christ; and though you have not seen Him, you love Him, and though you do not see Him now, but believe in Him, you greatly rejoice with joy inexpressible and full of glory, obtaining as the outcome of your faith the salvation of your souls" (1Pe. 1:3-9).

IN THE BOOK OF 2 PETER

His Divine Power Has Granted to Us Everything

"Simon Peter, a bond-servant and apostle of Jesus Christ, To those who have received a faith of the same kind as ours, by the righteousness of our God and Savior, Jesus Christ: Grace and peace be multiplied to you in the knowledge of God and of Jesus our Lord; seeing that His divine power has granted to us everything pertaining to life and godliness, through the true knowledge of Him who called us by His own glory and excellence. For by these He has granted to us His precious and magnificent promises, so that by them you may become partakers of the divine nature, having escaped the corruption that is in the world by lust. Now for this very reason also, applying all diligence, in your faith supply moral excellence, and in your moral excellence, knowledge, and in your knowledge, self-control, and in your self-control, perseverance, and in your perseverance, godliness, and in your godliness, brotherly kindness, and in your brotherly kindness, love. For if these qualities are yours and are increasing, they render you neither useless nor unfruitful in the true knowledge of our Lord Jesus Christ. For he who lacks these qualities is blind or short-sighted, having forgotten his purification from his former sins. Therefore, brethren, be all the more diligent to make certain about His calling and choosing you; for as long as you practice these things, you will never stumble; for in this way the entrance into the eternal kingdom of our

Lord and Savior Jesus Christ will be abundantly supplied to you" (2Pe. 1:1-11).

We Made Known to You the Power

"For we did not follow cleverly devised tales when we made known to you the power and coming of our Lord Jesus Christ, but we were eyewitnesses of His majesty. For when He received honor and glory from God the Father, such an utterance as this was made to Him by the Majestic Glory, "This is My beloved Son with whom I am well-pleased"—and we ourselves heard this utterance made from heaven when we were with Him on the holy mountain" (2Pe. 1:16-18).

IN THE BOOK OF REVELATION

Our God, to Receive Glory and Honor and Power

"After these things I looked, and behold, a door standing open in heaven, and the first voice which I had heard, like the sound of a trumpet speaking with me, said, 'Come up here, and I will show you what must take place after these things.' Immediately I was in the Spirit; and behold, a throne was standing in heaven, and One sitting on the throne. And He who was sitting was like a jasper stone and a sardius in appearance; and there was a rainbow around the throne, like an emerald in appearance. Around the throne were twenty-four thrones; and upon the thrones I saw twenty-four elders sitting, clothed in white garments, and golden crowns on their heads. Out from the throne come flashes of lightning and sounds and peals of thunder. And there were seven lamps of fire burning before the throne, which are the seven Spirits of God; and before the throne there was something like a sea of glass, like crystal; and in the center and around the throne, four living creatures full of eyes in front and behind. The first creature was like a lion, and the second creature like a calf, and the third creature had a face like that of a man, and the fourth creature was like a flying eagle. And the four living creatures, each one of them having six wings, are full of eyes around and within; and day and night they do not cease to say, 'HOLY, HOLY, HOLY is THE LORD GOD, THE ALMIGHTY, WHO WAS AND WHO IS AND WHO IS TO COME.' And when the living creatures give glory and honor and thanks to Him who sits on the throne, to Him who lives forever and ever, the twenty-four elders will fall down before Him who sits on the throne, and will worship Him who lives forever and ever, and will cast their crowns before the throne, saying, 'Worthy are You, our Lord and our God, to receive glory and honor and power; for You created all things, and because of Your will they existed, and were created'" (Rev. 4:1-11).

Worthy Is the Lamb to Receive Power, Riches, Wisdom, Might, Honor, Glory and Blessing

"Then I looked, and I heard the voice of many angels around the throne and the living creatures and the elders; and the number of them was myriads of myriads, and thousands of thousands, saying with a loud voice, 'Worthy is the Lamb that was slain to receive power and riches and wisdom and might and honor and glory and blessing.' And every created thing which is in heaven and on the earth and under the earth and on the sea, and all things in them, I heard saying, 'To

Him who sits on the throne, and to the Lamb, be blessing and honor and glory and dominion forever and ever.' And the four living creatures kept saying, 'Amen.' And the elders fell down and worshiped" (Rev. 5:11-14).

Honor and Power and Might, Be to Our God Forever

"After these things I looked, and behold, a great multitude which no one could count, from every nation and all tribes and peoples and tongues, standing before the throne and before the Lamb, clothed in white robes, and palm branches were in their hands; and they cry out with a loud voice, saying, 'Salvation to our God who sits on the throne, and to the Lamb.' And all the angels were standing around the throne and around the elders and the four living creatures; and they fell on their faces before the throne and worshiped God, saying, 'Amen, blessing and glory and wisdom and thanksgiving and honor and power and might, be to our God forever and ever. Amen'" (Rev. 7:9-12).

Your Great Reigning Power

"Then the seventh angel sounded; and there were loud voices in heaven, saying, 'The kingdom of the world has become the kingdom of our Lord and of His Christ; and He will reign forever and ever.' And the twenty-four elders, who sit on their thrones before God, fell on their faces and worshiped God, saying, 'We give You thanks, O Lord God, the Almighty, who are and who were, because You have taken Your great power and have begun to reign. And the nations were enraged, and Your wrath came, and the time came for the dead to be judged, and the time to reward Your bond-servants the prophets and the saints and those who fear Your name, the small and the great, and to destroy those who destroy the earth'" (Rev. 11:15-18).

Salvation, Power, Authority, and Kingdom of Christ

"And there was war in heaven, Michael and his angels waging war with the dragon. The dragon and his angels waged war, and they were not strong enough, and there was no longer a place found for them in heaven. And the great dragon was thrown down, the serpent of old who is called the devil and Satan, who deceives the whole world; he was thrown down to the earth, and his angels were thrown down with him. Then I heard a loud voice in heaven, saying, 'Now the salvation, and the power, and the kingdom of our God and the authority of His Christ have come, for the accuser of our brethren has been thrown down, he who accuses them before our God day and night. And they overcame him because of the blood of the Lamb and because of the word of their testimony, and they did not love their life even when faced with death. For this reason, rejoice, O heavens and you who dwell in them. Woe to the earth and the sea, because the devil has come down to you, having great wrath, knowing that he has only a short time'" (Rev. 12:7-12).

From the Glory of God and from His Power

"After these things I looked, and the temple of the tabernacle of testimony in heaven was opened, and the seven angels who had the seven plagues came out of the temple, clothed in linen, clean and bright, and girded around their chests with golden sashes. Then one of the four living creatures gave to the seven angels seven golden bowls full of the wrath of God, who lives forever and ever. And the temple was filled with smoke from the glory of God and from His power; and no one was able to enter the temple until the seven plagues of the seven angels were finished" (Rev. 15:5-8).

God Who Has the Power over These Plagues

"The fourth angel poured out his bowl upon the sun, and it was given to it to scorch men with fire. Men were scorched with fierce heat; and they blasphemed the name of God who has the power over these plagues, and they did not repent so as to give Him glory" (Rev. 16:8-9).

Hallelujah! Salvation, Glory and Power Belong to God

"After these things I heard something like a loud voice of a great multitude in heaven, saying, 'Hallelujah! Salvation and glory and power belong to our God; BECAUSE HIS JUDGMENTS ARE TRUE AND RIGHTEOUS; for He has judged the great harlot who was corrupting the earth with her immorality, and HE HAS AVENGED THE BLOOD OF HIS BOND-SERVANTS ON HER.' And a second time they said, 'Hallelujah! HER SMOKE RISES UP FOREVER AND EVER.' And the twenty-four elders and the four living creatures fell down and worshiped God who sits on the throne saying, 'Amen. Hallelujah!' And a voice came from the throne, saying, 'Give praise to our God, all you His bond-servants, you who fear Him, the small and the great.' Then I heard something like the voice of a great multitude and like the sound of many waters and like the sound of mighty peals of thunder, saying, 'Hallelujah! For the Lord our God, the Almighty, reigns. Let us rejoice and be glad and give the glory to Him, for the marriage of the Lamb has come and His bride has made herself ready.' It was given to her to clothe herself in fine linen, bright and clean; for the fine linen is the righteous acts of the saints" (Rev. 19:1-8).

DAILY FAITH CONFESSIONS

(These are not direct quotations from the Bible but are paraphrased confessions based on scripture.)

SAY THEM OUT LOUD.

I am God's child (Jn. 1:12). I am royalty (1 Pet. 2:9). I am hidden with Christ in God (Col. 3:3). I am united with the Lord (1 Cor. 6:17). I am a friend of Christ (Jn. 15:15). I am raised up with Him, and seated with Him in heavenly places in Christ Jesus (Eph. 2:6). I was bought with a price (1 Cor. 6:19-20). I am blessed when I come in, and blessed shall I be when I go out (Deut. 28:6). I am a personal witness of Christ (Acts 1:8). I am a saint who prays in the Holy Spirit to keep myself in the love of God (Jude 1:20-21). I draw near with confidence to the throne of grace (Heb. 4:16). I have been adopted by the Father (Eph. 1:5). I am the salt and light of the earth (Mt. 5:13). I am the head and not the tail, and I am above, and not underneath (Deut. 28:13). I have authority to trample serpents and scorpions and over all the power of the enemy (Lk. 10:19). I am a member of the body of Christ (1 Cor. 12:27). God blessed me to be fruitful, and multiply, and replenish the earth, and subdue it: and have dominion (Gen. 1:28). I cannot be separated from God's love (Ro. 8:39). The good work God has begun in me will be perfected (Phil. 1:5). I can do all things through Christ who strengthens me (Phil. 4:13). No weapon that is formed against me will prosper (Is. 54:17). So then faith cometh by hearing, and hearing by the word of God (Ro. 10:17 KJV). Faith is my currency to operate in the kingdom of God (Ro. 14:23). I am God's workmanship created in Christ Jesus for good works, which God prepared beforehand (Eph. 2:10). I have been appointed to bear fruit, and that my fruit would remain (Jn. 15:16). I am being wise when I am winning souls for King Jesus (Pr. 11:30). My body is the temple of the Holy Spirit (1 Cor. 6:19). I have access to God through the Holy Spirit (Eph. 2:18). I have been justified (Ro. 5:1). Therefore there is now no condemnation for those who are in Christ Jesus (Ro. 8:1). Greater is He who is in me than he who is in the world (1 Jn. 4:4). I will do greater works than Jesus because He went to the Father (Jn. 14:12). As God was with Moses, He will be with me; God will not fail me or forsake me (Jos. 1:5). I see myself the way God see me. God sees me as a king (Gen, 17:6, Rev. 1:6) God sees me as royalty (1 Pet. 2:9). God sees me as the righteousness of God in Christ, bold as a lion (Ro. 3:22, Pr. 28:1). God sees me without spot or wrinkle because of the blood of Jesus (1 Pet. 1:19). I am having faith for big things because God owns everything and I'm His son (Ps. 24:1). No man will be able to stand before me all the days of my life (Jos. 1:5). My Father is glorified by this that I bear much fruit, and proves I'm a disciple (see Jn. 15:8). I think big and confess big things because God is big (Ps. 24:1). I will respect God for the big God that He is and my mouth will create whatever I want (Lk. 6:45). I no longer think of millions, my renewed mind thinks of billions because the wealth of the wicked is laid up for the righteous (Pr. 13:22). The sinner's job is to gather and collect for the one who is good in God's sight (Ecc. 2:26). Redemption is not complete without prosperity. Jesus hung on the cross so I can have the whole package, not just salvation (2 Cor. 8:9). I don't have to qualify, Jesus has qualified me. Jesus reversed the curse. The devil is a liar, and Jesus is the Messiah. Jesus is made unto to me wisdom, righteousness, sanctification, and redemption (1 Cor. 1:30). I submit to God, I resist the devil and he flees from me (Jas. 4:7). For God has not given me the spirit of fear; but of power, and of love, and of a sound mind (2 Tim. 1:7). The Holy Spirit will teach me all things (Jn. 14:26). The Holy Spirit will guide me into all truth (Jn.16:13). The Holy Spirit abides in me, and I don't need anyone to teach me, but the anointing teaches me all things (1 Jn. 2:27). I quench fiery darts from the wicked one with the shield of faith (Eph. 6:16). I stand firm against the schemes of the devil (Eph. 6:11). I already have the victory and Satan cannot back me up. I hold my position of consistent victory after victory (2 Cor. 2:14). I walk in love and live by faith (Gal. 5:6). I have been redeemed from the curse of the law, poverty, sickness, and spiritual death (Gal. 3:13; Deut. 28). I will bear so much fruit. I'm God's workmanship created beforehand for good works (Eph. 2:10). God's favor is on my life (Ps. 3:8). God blesses me and His favor surrounds me as with a shield (Ps. 5:12). The kingdom of God is within me (Lk. 17:21). I have a production plant inside of me that bears fruit to change the world (Gen. 1:28). God gives me power to get wealth to establish His covenant on earth (Deut. 8:18). I am blessed to be a blessing (Gen. 12:2). I have Satan on the run. I will make a mockery of him (Jas. 4:7). I will spend forever in heaven with my King, Jesus Christ (2 Cor. 5:8). Thank you Father.

PRAYER FOR SALVATION

Say the following prayer out loud.

Heavenly Father, I am a sinner and I need a Savior. I confess Jesus Christ as the Lord of my life. I repent of all my sins. Father, I truly believe you raised Jesus from the dead. Father, give me spiritual hunger to spend time in Your Word day and night so my mind is renewed. I understand that by meditating and submitting to Your Word daily I will be transformed into the image of Jesus, day-by-day. Thank you, Father, for Your goodness, mercy, and grace. I pray in Jesus' name. Amen.

PRAYER FOR BAPTISM OF THE HOLY SPIRIT

Father, I am your child because Jesus is my Lord. Jesus said, "How much more shall your heavenly Father give the Holy Spirit to those who ask Him." I ask you now in the name of Jesus to fill me with the Holy Spirit. Thank you, Father, I received the baptism of the Holy Spirit by faith. I yield my vocal organs and expect to speak in tongues as the Holy Spirit gives me utterance in Jesus name. Father, I plan to pray in the Holy Spirit building myself up on my most holy faith, and keep myself in the love of God, as mentioned in Jude 20 and 21. In Jesus name I decree it. Amen.

ABOUT THE AUTHOR

Eugene Carvalho is the founder of Receiving by Faith. He is an administrator and Christian author of seventy-seven books. God uses him in the offices of pastor, evangelist and prophet. He holds a bachelor's degree in biblical studies and a double minor in pastoral ministry and world missions. He also holds a master's degree in practical theology. Eugene prayed for a translator and God sent his wife Mercedes who has a six- year degree in Spanish from a university in Tampico, Mexico. They have participated in evangelism in the streets of Mexico for many years. They have also traveled to churches all over the United States and Mexico winning souls and preaching faith. Their ministry website is: www.receivingbyfaith.org.

BOOKS BY EUGENE CARVALHO

To purchase other books by Eugene Carvalho visit receivingbyfaith.org or amazon.com.

Receiving by Faith
Faith for Every Day: 365 Daily Devotions
Faith Cometh by Hearing, and Hearing by the Word of God
Faith, Hope, and Love
Walk in Love and Live by Faith
Topical Christian Handbook and Scripture Guide
The Gospel Is the Power of God unto Salvation
Seed Time and Harvest Time
Your New Identity in Christ
The Cross and the Blood
The Holy Spirit
The Attributes of God
The Favor of God
The Glory of God
The Grace of God
The Power of God
The Promises of God
The Throne of God
The New Testament Church
Vengeance and Recompense
God's Angel's
Prayer and Fasting
God's Mighty Prophets
A Survey of Jesus Through the Epistles
The Names of Jesus
The Psalms of David

Old Testament Miracles
New Testament Miracles
Mountain Moving Confessions
Spiritual Formation: Unleashing the Kingdom of God Within You
Visions and Dreams
Prayer and Praise: The Big Artillery
Blessed Beyond Measure
Christ Heals: What the Bible Has to Say
My Peace I Give to You
Balancing Grace and Truth
Whereby, We Cry, Abba, Father
The Righteous Will Flourish like The Palm Tree
Be Strong and Courageous
Praise and Worship Changes Everything
Understanding the Importance of Authority
If You Are Willing and Obedient
Have Life More Abundantly
Sing Unto the Lord a New Song
The Power of the Tongue
The Supernatural: What the Bible Has to Say
The Truth Will Make You Free
Joy in the Holy Ghost
Praise Is Powerful: What the Bible Has to Say
Stewardship Regarding Our Finances
Love, Joy, and Peace Are Fruit of the Holy Ghost
Oh, Give Thanks to the Lord for He Is Good
The Kingdom of Heaven is at Hand
Acquiring Wisdom Is Vital
Grace and Mercy: What the Bible Has to Say
God Is Faithful: What the Bible Has to Say
God Is Love: What the Bible Has to Say

Trust and Obey

God's Feasts and Festivals

The God of Hope: What the Bible Has to Say

Pearls of Wisdom and Gems of Knowledge Regarding Christianity

Victory is Mine, Joy is Mine, Peace Is Mine: I Told Satan to Get Thee Behind

Apostles and Prophets: The Foundation of the Church

The Master's Gems

Striving Toward Perfection

For the Kingdom of God Is Righteousness, Peace and Joy in the Holy Ghost

Encountering Proverbs, Ecclesiastes, and Song of Solomon Through a Topical Survey

Prayer Is Powerful: What the Bible Has to Say

My People Are Destroyed By Lack of Knowledge

God Deserves Pure Worship

The Lord Requires Integrity: The Major Element of Leadership

A Topical Look at the Book of Deuteronomy

A Topical Look at the Book of Psalms

A Topical Look at the Book of Proverbs

A Topical Look at the Book of Isaiah

A Topical Look at the Book of John

A Topical Look at the Book of Hebrews

A Topical Look at the Book of Revelation

BOOKS BY EUGENE IN SPANISH

Las Promesas de Dios
Los Salmos de David
Lo Sobrenatural: Lo que la Bíblia Tiene que Decir
Una Mirada Topica Del Libro De Los Salmos
Dios es Amor: Lo que la Biblia Tiene que Decir
La Adquisición de la Sabiduría es Vital: Lo que la
Biblia Tiene que Decir

NOTES

NOTES

<u>NOTES</u>

www.ingramcontent.com/pod-product-compliance
Lightning Source LLC
Chambersburg PA
CBHW061712250726
48657CB00002B/600